FOLLOWING SEXUAL ABUSE

MARIE C. CROLL

Following Sexual Abuse

A Sociological Interpretation of Identity Re/Formation in Reflexive Therapy

UNIVERSITY OF TORONTO PRESS
Toronto Buffalo London

© University of Toronto Press Incorporated 2008
Toronto Buffalo London

www.utppublishing.com

Printed in Canada

ISBN 978-0-8020-9772-9 (cloth)

∞

Printed on acid-free paper

Library and Archives Canada Cataloguing in Publication

Croll, Marie Catharine
Following sexual abuse : a sociological interpretation of identity
re/formation in reflexive therapy / Marie C. Croll.

Includes bibliographical references and index.
ISBN 978-0-8020-9772-9

1. Sexual abuse victims – Rehabilitation – Case studies.   2. Sexual
abuse victims – Case studies.   3. Self – Social aspects.   4. Identity
(Psychology) – Social aspects.   5. Psychotherapy – Case studies.   I. Title.

RC560.S44C758 2008   616.85'836906   C2007-906002-1

University of Toronto Press acknowledges the financial assistance to its
publishing program of the Canada Council for the Arts and the Ontario
Arts Council.

University of Toronto Press acknowledges the financial support for its
publishing activities of the Government of Canada through the Book
Publishing Industry Development Program (BPIDP).

For Emma and Marta

I can't go on in any case. But I must go on ... So I'll go on. All very fine, but the voice is failing, it's the first time, no, I've been through that, it has even stopped, many a time, that's how it will end again, I'll go silent, for want of air, then the voice will come back and I'll begin again. My voice. The voice.

– Samuel Beckett, The Unnameable

Contents

Acknowledgments

I most gratefully acknowledge and thank the four women who gave permission for their accounts to be told here. I am indebted as well to the many other courageous women who spent months and sometimes years telling me their stories.

This would not have been completed without the unbending encouragement and practical support of Rainer Baehre.

I am deeply and lovingly indebted to Ann Millar, who first introduced me to the importance of dreams.

My extra-special appreciation goes to Marta and Emma Croll-Baehre, who came along together in the middle of this work and most lovingly and understandingly permitted me to finish.

I owe many thanks to Sue Scott for her wise and gentle guidance and practical support.

Finally, I wish to express my gratitude to Memorial University's Aid to Scholarly Publishing Programme for their generous publication subvention grant.

FOLLOWING SEXUAL ABUSE

Introduction

My former career as a therapist brought me into contact with numerous clients, most of whom were women. This clientele ranged in age from eleven to sixty-two. They represented a diverse educational background, and they reflected a socio-economic cross-section of the Newfoundland population. The great majority of them had sustained sexual exploitation in one form or another. The accounts of their injuries, a selection of which have been gathered here, were all well known to me before I embarked on this sociological study. And as these sequestered experiences accumulated into a collection of narratives in my private keeping, I aimed to give them a greater profile. In short, my desire to give my former clients a sociological representation of their accounts is the principal motivation for writing this book. By probing our therapeutic observations and discoveries from the perspective of social research, I recognized I could contribute to a fuller awareness of an often strictly personal and solitary suffering. This sociological application of my therapeutic findings also makes possible a re-conceptualization of what had become for me a familiar – if not by then also an exhausted – theoretical terrain.

When I first decided to bring these sociologically important accounts out of a secluded therapeutic context, it was to better understand, describe, and disseminate what consistently appeared to succeed in the therapeutic process, as my clients essentially reinvented themselves and found ways to reintegrate themselves into their social worlds. As a practitioner I recognized that the telling was for many of my clients an act of reparation. This posed the research question: how did this evolution happen? From the therapeutic perspective, I have observed it. My role in this process was essential and clear to me. My judgement about what was happening was a bricolage incorporating subjective, intuitive, experiential, and reflexive components. Informed by these perspectives, I worked alongside my clients and lightly guided them as they reshaped themselves in the wake of profound personal disintegration. This therapeutic work consistently revealed that my clients passed from an intrapersonal revision of their experience through narrative to an interpersonal acceptance of their account.

This is precisely the point at which the insights of therapy became fuelled by the observations of social theory. I saw that the interpersonal and social experience of reconstructing oneself following trauma represented something much wider-reaching than sexual abuse, and I considered this phenomenon to be of consequence to intellectual audiences beyond the therapeutic community. In particular, I wanted to gain deeper insight into the interaction between intrapersonal and social worlds by examining the creation of personal accounts formed in the therapeutic dialogue. This I achieved by selectively applying primarily sociological but also anthropological and, more peripherally, literary studies to these self-constructions. Foremost, I found studies in feminist sociology, reflexivity, and symbolic interactionism most helpful in my search for a clearer understanding of the nature of sexual abuse, trauma, identity reconstruction through narrative, and the bridging of private and social worlds.

When I began my academic career in earnest, studying English literature at the graduate level, I was drawn to symbols and how the symbolic is expressed, as I still am. My move to the study and then practice of therapy was a logical leap because I could pursue my interest in the symbolic as it was expressed in the construction and reparation of self. All the while I remained fascinated with how and to what extent these symbolic personal reconstructions were fused with social and cultural environments. This abiding interest finally led me to pursue doctoral work in sociology.

This book then encompasses two interwoven pursuits in which I, as a therapist and sociologist, have participated. One pursuit is represented in the analysis of therapeutic accounts collected from a sample of sexually abused clients. To state their experiences in the broadest terms, they achieved differing levels of personal reintegration following atrocious intimate violations. Their personal reparation was accomplished in varying levels only after their experiences were addressed in a reflexive therapeutic dialogue. Through their own creative processes of restructuring their lives, especially in their use of dream metaphors and narratives, these clients developed a new understanding of themselves through a therapeutic process in which they played an integral role.

The other pursuit represents my experience as a researcher and applied sociologist. As a participant (much like a 'participant observer') and mediator of my clients' reconstructions, I analysed their accounts from two perspectives – a therapist's and a sociologist's. My training and thinking as a therapist and my portrayal of clients' experiences in therapy was the first area of professional expertise, while the second – my work as a sociologist – reflects my present research perspective. This sociological standpoint necessitated a dialogic and inductive reinterpretation of what I had observed as a therapist, and a view of these individual accounts through a different disciplinary lens. I have for that reason compiled, analysed, synthesized, and explicated this material from a social research angle. The application of sociological and cultural understandings to therapeutic findings led me to investigate clients' processes of forming and communicating their most personal content and the wider social and reciprocal effect that making their experiences public had on their accounts.

The importance of defining the largely uncharted and apparently obscure transmissions between the intrapersonal self and the social one is a fertile area for social theorists and practitioners. Charles Lemert recognized that this level of social interchange contains sociology's essence: 'The beauty of poetry, as of sociology, is in the soul's ability to join the personal and the local with the disjointed differences of the social whole' (2002, viii). My microanalysis of personal accounts extends his observation by encapsulating and grounding a vital struggle for connection between 'intrapersonal' and 'social' experiences. Sociological and therapeutic literature has often presented these internal and external processes as apparently quite separate. However, my clients' accounts demonstrate that each experience intersects with the other, so that neither is distinctly detached.

This research, then, in its broadest form, addresses the conditions under which commonly supported constructions of reality become reflected in the changing consciousness of self. My evidentiary base is the clients' evolving self-description, through their accounts or narratives, as it broadened from their internalized perceptions to encompass external views of themselves. Within this context, I came to compare social and therapeutic descriptions of self, how they are formed, how they are reflexively transformed, and how they are symbolically mediated. Likewise, as a sociologist, I explored the results of my own pursuit as therapist and social researcher, in an effort to analyse and explain how my clients' accounts were shaped, and why.

Objectification and Exploitation: Several Feminist Considerations

My clientele consisted primarily of girls and women whose physical and sexual experiences of exploitation and violation had been perpetrated against them by men. It follows that one of the primary elements of sexual abuse, as I observed it and as other research has substantiated, is its overwhelming gender-related basis (Finkelor 1986a, 1986b), because women constitute an institutionally and culturally oppressed group. My approach views sex and gender as pivotal to understanding all other issues and is best suited to working with and researching female clients who are attempting to resolve problems that grew directly out of manipulation, personal injury, and the misuse of power, almost always by men.

It is difficult to find therapeutic abuse literature that does not reflect on gender issues, because feminist interpretations pervade and indeed define the subject. Therapist Jan Ellis writes, for example, 'My basic assumption in working with women in therapy is that all of us have been abused. No one escapes the world's prevailing attitude that women and children are less valuable than adult males' (1990, 243). This message also infuses much feminist research in the social sciences. Suzanne Pharr, for instance, locates sexism and violence against women, not as individual problems to be treated as therapeutic issues but rather as politically and socially entrenched ones.

> Women have not wanted to hear battered women say that the verbal abuse was as harmful as the physical abuse: to acknowledge that truth would be tantamount to acknowledging that virtually every woman is a battered woman. It is difficult to keep strong against accusations of being a bitch, stupid, inferior, etc., etc. It is especially difficult when these individual assaults are backed up by a society that shows women in textbooks, advertising, TV programs, movies, etc., as debased, silly, inferior, and sexually objectified, and a society that gives tacit approval to pornography. When we internalize these messages, we call the result 'low self-esteem,' a therapeutic individualized term. It seems to me we should use the more political expression: when we internalize these messages, we experience internalized sexism, and we experience it in common with all women liv-

ing in a sexist world. The violence against us is supported by a society in which woman-hating is deeply embedded. (Pharr 2003, 504)

The subject, as Pharr's emphasis indicates, fits quite necessarily into a broader social and political context, and its remedies are socially manifested.

Yet such sociological and therapeutic analyses of sexual exploitation, like Pharr's and Ellis's, rarely turn to the perspective of intrapersonal reconstructions for additional insight. In bypassing this level of personal experience and interpretation, however, social researchers neglect critical components of the reparation. As my study demonstrates, the intimate and micro-level of establishing meaning provides subtle, symbolic, and crucial insights that the macro-view alone cannot, yet it is here that possible remedies exist.

The analytical direction that I adopt in investigating intrapersonal experience as a way to understanding the social objectification of women has already been initiated by Dorothy Smith and others. Smith, in particular, has called for social research to investigate the micro-experiences of women. In *The Everyday World as Problematic*, she contends that women's experience 'has not been represented in the making of our culture.' She is convinced that, for women, 'there is a gap between where we are and the means we have to express and act' (1987, 19–20). Smith candidly punctuates the consequences of women's exclusion from the making of culture as their 'lack of authority to speak' (85). Yet the danger in this, one that I have seen affecting my clients, is that 'women's means to reflect upon themselves is a reflection from outside themselves, the structuring of themselves not as subjects, but as other' (51). Through the course of reflexive therapy, a reinterpretation of my clients' notions of sexuality and equality was often necessary in order for them to reaffirm and/or reconstruct their self-identity, especially in a world where their existence had often been devoid of personal boundaries and a firm sense of who they were.

Feminist sociology has often validated and contextualized the kinds of reconstructions my clients independently undertook. Specifically, it has provided a better understanding for women within the framework of a man-made environment that, as Sheila Rowbotham notes, was not constructed to make sense to them: 'We had no means of reflecting our inner selves to an outer movement of things. All theory, all connecting language and ideas which could make us see ourselves in relation to a continuum or as a part of a whole were external to us. We had no part in their making' (1973, 30).

Similar observations underscore my clients' therapeutic accounts, which fill the representational gap to which Rowbotham and Smith refer. When they located unconsciously rendered words and symbols that were encompassing and adequate enough to describe their experiences, they were able to stand apart from the dominant and external depictions of their experiences and represent themselves. Governing discourses define my clients, often mostly inaccurately, and untangling them from external projections, at least where their sexual violation is concerned, becomes a therapeutic strategy. Primarily, throughout therapy, we became engaged in the reclamation and interpretation of the clients' experiences, as expressed in their own words and metaphors.

Elaine Neil Orr has located in the poet Tillie Olsen's words the essence of our therapeutic endeavour: 'Silence is metaphoric of unredeemed loss, while voice, regardless of how feeble, inarticulate, and unheeded, symbolizes the hope of recovery and the promise of signification' (1987, 142). This silence is the very situation that my clients, feminist scholars, and others have attempted to redress. It is this 'feeble' and 'unheeded' voice that the therapeutic exchange seeks to draw out and fortify.

Such unheeded voices have been theoretically revived in feminist standpoint theory (Gilligan 1982; Hartsock 1998, Stanley 1990). Smith summarizes this standpoint as 'a method that, at the onset of inquiry, creates the space for an absent subject, and an absent experience that is to be filled with the presence and spoken experience of actual women speaking of and in the actualities of their everyday worlds' (1987, 107). The accounts emanating from my clients' material realities help to reintegrate otherwise lost voices and place them into sociological awareness. As such, an interpretation of meaning from lived experience has assumed a key place in my case studies of girls and women. It has become central in translating the unfolding dynamics of my practice and placing my findings into analytical social research. Viewing my clients' abuses from a gendered and situated perspective has illuminated social marginalization and lack of self-authority. Social theory and praxis have become integral to my thinking about the therapist–client relationship. When I was holding up my clients' sexual violations to analysis, feminist social perspectives helped depersonalize their abuses and, in turn, alleviated some of their associated guilt. They provided a framework for the client from within which to address underlying issues of equality, empowerment, and authority. In this manner, we borrowed from a collective feminist voice and analysis, while the previously silenced voices of my clients and their lack of comprehension gained strength and understanding.

Case Studies: Transcribing Inner Experience

I began my therapeutic practice in Newfoundland during the early 1990s after a decade of growing interest in child sexual abuse (Bagley 1984; Finkelhor 1984, 1986, 1989; Kelly 1988a, 1988b; Schlesinger 1986), and shortly after the public revelations of abuse of generations of boys within the province's Roman Catholic orphanage for boys – Mount Cashel became widely known and had a major impact on public perception (Harris 1990). Initially, public exposure of sexual misconduct by Irish-Canadian clergy, as documented first in the Winter Commission (Archdiocese of St John's 1990) and then in the Hughes Inquiry (Hughes 1991) resulted in police investigations, yet press releases revealing abuse at this orphanage at first produced little public reaction. With the televised trial of a great many Christian Brothers who were alleged to have physically and sexually abused boys over decades, the province, and indeed the entire nation, took notice. The events at the orphanage subsequently triggered disclosure of other sexual abuse throughout the province (Rogers 1992). A year after the large scale-revelations, a victim from Mount Cashel arrived at my practice. The fallout from these abuses is still socially evident in Newfoundland.

Clients have come to me from a multitude of sources including the Department of Social Services, employee assistance programs, the Newfoundland Constabulary, law offices, physicians, and clients' self-referral. The majority, however, were sent to me through the Victim Services Branch of the provincial Department of Justice. My request to research and write the stories of clients referred to me by the department – all victims of crimes who had filed charges against their assailants – was denied out of concern about confidentiality and lengthy, unsettled court trials. While I have been forced to exclude their accounts, they reflected much of what my other clients experienced.

This research was a reflexive endeavour. Researcher and subject continuously reflected on the experiences of one another and in the process altered one another. Jane Elliot, in weighing reflexivity in the context of a 'crisis of representation,' rightly contends that narrative research is necessarily co-constructed. She says, 'Once we become aware that when the subjects of our research provide us with narratives, they are not merely reporting their experiences but rather are engaged in an activity that makes sense of those experiences, we are obliged to admit that our own research narratives are also constructed' (2005, 154). In accepting the interdependent, subjective, and co-structured status of this undertaking, I nevertheless attempted to relay my clients' projects of reparation from their perspective and, where possible, in their words.

The gathering and representation of these accounts produced a degree of melding practice with research. That blending was unavoidable and perhaps inevitable (and not unwelcome). Through the collaboration between therapist/researcher and client, there has been an overlapping of our ideas, expectations, and/or analyses, with mutual insights derived from our interaction. In this sense, our pursuits intersected.

The information gleaned, recorded, and expressed in the accounts of my clients is presented as a series of case studies – a therapeutic and sociological tool of analysis. The individual instances of sexual exploitation, which I also see in collective terms, consist of personal revelations that fit, though imperfectly, into the definition of a case study. Denzin says that a case 'may describe an event, a process, or a person,' and that it may incorporate 'the analysis of a single case or of multiple instances of the same process as it is embodied in the life experiences of a community, a group, or a person' (1989, 34). This definition, with its emphasis on process as opposed to ordered biographical detail, captures the varieties of 'inner experience' that I have uncovered in my practice and that I describe in the following chapters. Framed in this way, case study work brings the reader into the very centre of the client's role in therapy and also extends the case beyond the individual to the lives of the many others who have been similarly exploited.

I have drawn heavily on four selected cases for this project that quintessentially reflect my style of reflexive therapy and close therapeutic analysis. They demonstrate the long-term commitment to reconstruction that was usual with my clients, and typify the depth of exploration undertaken during a lengthy period of therapy. Each case represents years of contact. Once these cases were chosen, I made yet a further selection of what to include or exclude from my clients' accounts. This graduated process of selection was like Elliot's notion of narrative research as a construction. It was only through such a discriminatory process that I could describe and analyse the nature and complexity of the therapeutic work in which my clients and I engaged. Such selection of course was limiting, but it was also necessary. As Denzin aptly comments, 'There is no way to stuff a real-live person between the two covers of a text' (1989, 83). I must add, however, that the words included from therapeutic diary entries and conversations are my clients', entirely unedited.

There were also ethical considerations to weigh while I was transcribing my clients' therapeutic processes. To begin, my two interests – therapeutic practice and sociological research – sometimes created competing agendas. A most apparent illustration lay in my decision to use client accounts as a methodological basis. While these studies held great value as research material, the public rendering of accounts that had been given in confidence posed a potential ethical dilemma. I therefore decided to ask permission to use the accounts of only those clients who had terminated therapy. This eradicated completely my concern about influencing the ongoing therapeutic process. In seeking permission to make their accounts public, I presented each former client with a release form, which we read together and discussed. At that time I expressed some ethical concerns, including my request for their participation in this research, for none of them had entered therapy knowing that they would be asked to have their private conversations taken beyond the consultation room. Here was one point where my researcher role and my role as therapist collided.

Included in our deliberations was the matter of client loss of power and control, and the risks (despite the use of pseudonyms and all efforts to disguise personal details) of clients being identified, should this work be locally disseminated. I then insisted, because some nevertheless wanted to grant their permission immediately, that they take more time to reconsider any possible personal ramifications that releasing this information might have. This, I hoped, would temper lingering feelings of vulnerability or a sense of obligation in assenting to my request. In meeting again to consider any thoughts and feelings that my proposal might have motivated, each client was, without exception, firm in her resolve to commit her account to this research. Most of them expressed, if anything, an even stronger desire to have their story shared in the hope that they might enlighten practitioners or offer support to other victims. At this point, in response to the only concern that was ever expressed by these women, I also reassured each client that I would make every effort to disguise her true identity. I then suggested that each choose a symbolically significant name drawn from our work together that would represent her in the book.

Their inclination to share these stories of sexual trauma was surprisingly strong. As a therapist, however, I recognized that these accounts might not be entirely anonymous if used as research data. I also knew that making public a private experience could disturb my clients. And as a researcher I sensed that meaningful life experiences could not be lifted magically and without disruption from their human context. Despite these apprehensions, I decided, with my clients' assurances, to employ this invaluable evidence as research material.

The stories ultimately included represent a cross section of sexual exploitation accounts. These encased, in-depth narratives allow for an accurate representation of the issues, problems, and experiences arising from sexual exploitation, as the clients themselves expressed it. In the following chapters one account primarily describes incest by a father, a second involves the gang rape of a teenager, and another tells of childhood incest by both a brother and a grandfather as well as of other sexual assaults by neighbouring men. A final narrative deals with a woman's struggle to reformulate her identity in the face of solid recollections of sexual abuse and many missing memories. This final chapter probes a client's conflicted response to missing memory and the widespread public tendency to dismiss such incomplete or conflicting memories of sexual abuse. The ordering of these narratives is also quite deliberate for another reason. Collectively, they have been positioned to give the reader a clear impression and basic understanding of the therapeutic course that many of my clients followed. I use these representative accounts to highlight the essential stages that most pass through. Placing these accounts in separate chapters also accentuates the order and process of my own evolution as a therapist and social researcher, and it helps to explain to the reader the insights that refined my therapeutic approach.

In this sense, the first case that presents childhood incest experiences links the publicly construed notion of 'survival' with the private experience and shows how the client often bridges the gap between private and public by directing our focus to the interrelationship between the 'textually mediated' (Smith 1990b, 210) representation of her experience and her subjective reality.

The second account is of the rape of a teenager and it highlights the reflexive and private nature of the reconstruction undertaken in therapy following a violent and invasive physical and sexual attack. This narrative demonstrates what happens after a client has incorporated the public perceptions of what has occurred to her, keeping what is useful and shedding what is not. This chapter investigates how insights spawn an original and potentially productive self-reconstruction. This happens by revising the account and recognising that internally rendered processes, such as dreaming and the epiphany, can be adapted into a working script. Bringing to light the creative and subjective aspects of the therapeutic process punctuates the distinctiveness of the work that my clients undertake. For many, this internal work gives them a necessary channel to express their own insights while momentarily releasing them from the public gaze.

The third case study reveals a child's experiences of incest and sexual abuse. Her intimate social world was not prepared to hear of her incest and sexual assault, yet she developed a powerful need to speak of it. I bring this representative account into the spotlight in order to demonstrate the interrelationship between storytelling and the reception of such accounts. The painstakingly slow retelling in therapy symbolizes the gap that often exists between the need to tell and the personal and public resistance to hearing it. This particular narrative also asks us how we reconnect ourselves – after a time of alienation and fragmentation – to a collective identity that had denied our reality. It also asks us to explore our sensitivity (or lack of it) to such subjective accounts in an age where we are often bombarded in the media with personal narratives.

The final case study is an account of a woman with fragmented memories of possible sexual assaults and incest. It highlights questions such as truth and reliability that confront all who have been sexually abused as well as those who work with them in their reparation. The 'truth' of the sexual exploitation experience, in the form that many of my clients eventually incorporate, takes us far from the textually mediated perception of truth. Clients usually reject externally imposed views and reclaim their self-descriptions only when they are embodied, gendered, symbolic, multifaceted, and authentic. This reclamation of a more complex self, in turn, restores authorship to their individual experiences and contributes fundamentally to their reconstruction.

In recounting and reconstructing these experiences, the point where each woman places her emphasis renders each account unique. These narratives differ not so much in their central themes but in what each woman locates and defines as that part of her account or self that most needs addressing and reconstructing in the wake of her violations. Distinctive too is how she determines her strategy. This need to rebuild the self following abuse is common yet is also unique to each individual. It is at once a process through which each individual must pass alone and out of which she can locate personal meaning.

Personal Meaning, Public Words

How do we interpret the impressions made by the social world upon the private person? How are such influences uncovered in therapy? To begin, all my clients suffered abuses not of their own making, and, they subsequently, and to their disadvantage, had these personal experiences interpreted for them through words, and indeed a discourse that was not of their own construction. Externally imposed ideologies alienated them and contributed to a further loss of self. However, as their accounts demonstrate, personal dream symbols and how they were expressed infused my clients with a sense of personal agency. Dream analysis satisfied their sense of authenticity, which, in turn, advanced an emotional resolution. Our mutual endeavour thus converged in reintegrating the clients by these means, and by reconstructing them by making them central to their own accounts.

This therapeutic work, interpreted through a selective application of social research, contributes to sociological analysis by providing a valuable distillation of gendered and communicative conflicts and analysing the interplay between the individual and the social. In its emphasis on individual internal development, the therapeutic process demands a tremendous degree of privacy and introspection. Nevertheless, while each of my clients had experienced some degree of social separation, they all needed also to participate in a social world, because none were functioning in a vacuum or completely self-contained. Ken Plummer notes, 'Isolated individuals and abstract societies are there none' (1995, 20). Nor would their therapeutic alliance have been fruitful if we had crafted an artificial atmosphere that split personal from social. In fact, the need to integrate external social perceptions and external descriptions of their abuse, based upon a desire for eventual reconciliation with their social worlds, constituted the primary underlying motivation for my clients to be in therapy and directly and indirectly stimulated their insights. Consequently, my clients' narratives denote the avenue they used to negotiate the 'how to' of self-construction and of social construction, linking private and public worlds.

Prior to therapy, all those whose accounts I explore were aware that their lives had not belonged to them. They had endured a profound sense of indignity and a loss of trust in others as a result of externally

inflicted abuses. The consequent and acute perception of marginalization had relegated them to the periphery of their social worlds and
immobilized their willingness and ability to communicate with others
about their abuse. In many instances, the desire to disown their original
stories, ones that defined them unwillingly, had become so compelling
as to fuel suicide attempts, substance and food abuse, violent relationships, and other self-destructive behaviours.

These women also shared a deep awareness that those closest to
them, those who were supposed to protect them, including authority
figures, had failed to do so at a most critical juncture. This consistent
and abiding sense of social desertion and most private betrayal was, in
one sense, why I came to consider their private troubles as public
issues. For all of my clients, their previous abuse contributed to a long-
term severance of trust in others, and this situation contributed to
often unwanted social isolation, or worse. Society, in other words, had
made them strangers. Their subsequent involvement in a therapeutic
researching of self demonstrated that this was not who they wanted to
be. Their yearning for social affirmation and understanding, as it was
expressed in counselling, was demonstrated first by their pursuit of a
mutually engaged as opposed to a neutral witness/therapist.

My role in this pursuit of affirmation correspondingly heightened
my awareness of how externally produced perspectives affected my clients and intersected with their intra-personal notion of self. Over and
above their quest to redefine their experience, these clients sought reconciliation, a symbolic and internal one at first and then an interpersonal one, through which they hoped to restore trusting relationships
both at the personal and collective levels. In analysing this comprehensive reintegration of self-identity I engaged reflexivity as an investigative tool that therapists and sociologists have in some important
respects interpreted quite similarly.

Reflexive transformation is a circular process of engendering awareness and fostering regeneration that is consistently directed back upon
itself. To place this into the context of my work, I discovered that as
clients' accounts took form in therapy, they began to spontaneously
operate within a reflexive cycle in which both internally and externally
rendered constructions fed into their self-shaping productions. This
reflexive process brought us quite consistently back to a social perspective. In light of this transformation, I recognized that the subjective
and often symbolic work of a self-consciously reflexive therapeutic approach had much to offer to social and cultural theorists who are inter-

ested in that threshold between the 'subjective' or inner world – the mostly unrecorded experiences of therapy – and the well-documented 'objective' or social world – the structural, the public, the external world – to which my clients sought a return. My clients' accounts therefore functioned as 'narratives of identity' (Hinchman and Hinchman 1997, xvii) through which each client reconsidered themselves in an unremitting negotiation with a dominant and external discourse.

Edward Bruner says, 'Stories make meaning' (1997, 265). I'd like to pursue this point for a moment. Narratives are essentially reflexive endeavours, because in constructing the self in what is basically a creative process, they can bring about social transformation within the individual. In turn, each account construction alters how that individual is then perceived from without, and finally how that changed person effects her broader social environment. In much the same way, our necessarily feminist-oriented therapeutic process worked closely with the self-referential experience of recreating oneself after that self had been described and, in large part, constructed by external sources. For the client, account reconstruction involves an active researching and consequent reinterpretation of herself, in opposition to the dominant, primarily patriarchal, discourses that have, in a sense, colonized her sense of reality and understanding of self. Reflexivity, as methodology, admits into the realm of sociological discourse my clients' perceptions of their experiences. It acknowledges and honours the significant, in-depth, and often symbolic process of individual transformation in therapy following sexual exploitation.

To illustrate, Barbara Myerhoff views the researcher/therapist's work as necessarily one that focuses on 'clarification of the relationship between the subject and the introjected voices of society.' In her view, the researcher reflects the self to the subject, 'formally and informally, providing a corrective lens, and sometimes realigning components of the self' (1992, 356). Through exchanges between the researcher and the researched, those researched then also become collaborators in the research project because both the researcher/therapist's and the client's considerations become the product of two persons reflecting upon one another and thereby influence and change one another's understanding. In the following chapters, my clients' accounts demonstrate that such a witnessed introspection was critical in providing them with a degree of separation from the dominant cultural view of that experience. They illustrate too that, as soon as their intrapersonal understandings began to seek an interpersonal reflection, a socially manifested reflexivity was set in motion.

The client's process of externalization often goes something like this. In the wake of her first expression of what had happened, she uses internally rendered symbols to reformulate that experience, which is defined by the client and therapist together, and departs from the pre-existing vocabulary upon which she relied to make sense of that experience. Already, at this early stage, her perceptions of herself and of what had happened were one step removed from 'pure' experience. Following such initial attempts to articulate her situation, we, client and therapist, drew upon dreams and symbolic reference points on the premise that such imagery contributes content that is less contrived and less accessible to external manipulation. Most importantly for the client, this imagery – her own imagery – framed in her own words reminded her of personal agency and validity. This stage in the therapy underscored for me the fact that there are significant associations between the intrapersonal identification of symbols and social and cultural interpretations of the symbolic construction and presentation of self. In fact, and most significantly, the client's isolated work on the self was often inadequate or incomplete until her reconstructed self was socially recognized or legitimated.

Identity construction and its place in narrative research have been well surveyed by Hinchman and Hinchman (1997). In exploring the wide range of interdisciplinary perspectives that have staked claims in narrative theory, these authors note its appeal to narrative therapists, dream researchers, and psychologists inspired by symbolic interactionism. Of particular significance is their description of George Herbert Mead's conception of identity as 'created rather than already present and waiting to be discovered.' From this perspective, the self is regarded as 'a protean entity that is continually being formed and shaped through narrative' (Hinchman and Hinchman 1997, 120–1). My own in-depth work with identity construction in clients' accounts draws indirectly from Mead's contributions and demonstrates this to be a most apt general description of how identities are constituted and reconstituted.

Subsequently, understanding at a micro-level how selfhood is mediated led me to view this process in broader social terms, in which symbolic interactionism (discussed below), in combination with reflexive narrativity and feminist analysis, became an invaluable hybrid investigative tool. Both the reflexive and symbolic interactionist perspectives deliberate on the client's multifaceted self – those aspects that Norman K. Denzin (1992) characterizes as the phenomenological, interactional, linguistic, and ideological dimensions that constitute the biography of

the person. They consider the underlying symbolic forms and exchanges of social experience rather than seeking out only 'objective'
content or pursuing 'literal' interpretations. Together, the reflexive perspective and symbolic interactionism enabled me to reflect upon my
clients' expressions and upon the self-identities that they grew to claim
as more authentically their own.

Symbolic Communication: Private and Social

Symbolic interactionist David Maines contends that 'one of the great
benefits of focusing on narratives is that they are one form of communication, and by conceptualizing sociology narratively, we are forced to
take communication very seriously' (1993, 14). The symbolic interactionist framework allows an analysis and explanation of that symbolic
communication within the context of a sociological discourse, and provides the terms by which such interactions have come to be defined and
understood. Specifically, symbolic interactionism appropriates and
integrates 'a living social symbol' and places it at the very centre of the
ongoing discourse and debate on narrative development and human
communication. For my purposes, this emphasis establishes a point of
intersection between a therapeutic practice and a social analysis. The
identity reconstructed through the therapeutic account provides its creator with a subjective sense of self-continuity as it symbolically integrates the events of lived experience in the plot of the story the client
relays about her life.

   In reflecting upon this unfolding dynamic, I became attracted to the
constructionist and thus potentially emancipatory elements of symbolic interactionism, because of the way that interactionists see the levels at which expression of intrapersonal, interpersonal, and social are
symbolically and reflexively created and interactive. This multilayered
approach offered a road into such postmodernist but also significantly
therapeutic problems as 'the "I am" of existence, which is separate from
the "I am" of meaning' (Lacan 1990, 108). In this regard, salient personal transformations, as viewed by Denzin, for instance, stem from
interactional situations in which the private self is spontaneously rede-
fined in the face of a larger social crisis. This symbolic perspective on
identity construction is well suited to the work of reparation and integration towards which we (client and therapist together) had continually worked.

   My clients' accounts represented isolated attempts at intrapersonal integrity and continuity that, in turn, sought a social reception. Denzin's perspective on communication underscores my attraction to the broader implications of this process. It is an analytical bridge between intrapersonal and social experiences. In highlighting communication as a symbolic process, Denzin extends an analysis developed by James Carey, that the communicative process is one wherein 'reality is produced, maintained, repaired and transformed,' as my clients' experiences of therapy also consistently demonstrated (Carey 1989, 5; cited in Denzin 1989, 98). In his search for a deeper understanding of the social, Carey also focused on that inner realm of experience, much like the one my clients and I had sought out. His analytical 'gaze' turned inward, as did ours, in pursuit of what he calls a 'more substantial domain of existence' (1989, 25).

Carey seeks to lend expression to the nuances and the ritual nature of a complex process of symbol-making that frequently goes unheeded, believing that 'reality is brought into existence, is produced by the construction, apprehension, and utilization of symbolic forms' (1989, 25). It is his contention that the social sciences 'can take the most obvious yet background facts of social life and force them into the foreground of wonderment' (24). It is precisely in the spirit suggested by Carey that I have now contributed to social research – through the very local material that I have gathered, fostered, and often symbolically reinterpreted with my clients, as we probed the subtleties of their private experiences and communicative exchanges, which jointly brought about important self-revelations. Social and cultural understandings and applications of symbols have advanced my understanding of my clients' sense of self within their peopled worlds and have from a sociological perspective provided me with a vocabulary for interpreting my counselling work. Within our therapeutic exchanges, symbols provided a way of giving coherence and representation to what was spontaneously rendered and 'inexpressible.' As an alternative to an externally derived perspective, the symbol, as it was drawn out of dreams for explication, acted as a further means of expression.

Yet the public conventions and the points of interchange within any spoken exchange are also social, symbolic, and crucial to both our private work in therapy and in social exchanges generally. It was the role and application of symbolism, as a vital form of communication, that I explicated to find the common ground between the personal and social symbol. The self-conscious and private symbolic interaction of therapy functions separately from the symbolic exchanges of the client's broader social and cultural world. In short, it assumes a different dimension of communication. The therapeutic exchange, that mediation between private and social worlds, represents a deliberately constructed relationship in which spontaneously recovered symbols are given coherence and aid communication.

While symbols provide an exact and crystallized form of communication, perhaps because of their subjective origins and qualities, they are also a form of social transmission that is still much overlooked in sociology. This intentional oversight may well be rooted in the reasons given by Ian Burkitt for what he sees as the social sciences' exclusion of 'the body' as a site of serious research. He suggests that the body has been marginalized 'because it tended to be thought of as unruly and unpredictable, the seat of the emotions and passions, things which cannot be calculated or represented in any regular way' (1999, 1). In spite of these problems, Burkitt advocates a sociological consideration of the body and self.

Burkitt's standpoint is one that reflects my own interests in understanding both my clients' embodied existence and their unconscious productions. He argues for 'a multi-dimensional approach to the body and the person which conceives of human beings as complexes composed of both the material and the symbolic' (1999, 2). I also share this view. In order to comprehend and work effectively with my clients' visions of themselves – visions shaped by others' perceptions of them – it was fruitful to assimilate a 'multi-dimensional' perspective. Accordingly, my study and its representation of clients' symbolic, physical, and inner-personal pursuits towards unity encompass various dimensions of being. My findings reinforce the idea that the experience of intra- and interpersonal fragmentation and the unification of inner and outer realms of experience must not be limited to the psychoanalytic milieu.

Berger and Luckmann shared this concern with a multi-level approach to understanding selfhood. They were interested in sources of meaning that went beyond the social yet remained connected to it. The following excerpt from The Social Construction of Reality captures the significance and scope of the connection between the symbolic, the individual, and the social, as they saw it.

The symbolic universe is conceived of as the matrix of all socially objectivated and subjectively real meanings; the entire historic society and the entire biography of the individual are seen as events taking place within this universe. What is particularly important, the marginal situations of the life of the individual (marginal, that is, in not being included in the reality of everyday existence in society) are also encompassed by the symbolic universe. Such situations are experienced in dreams and fantasies as provinces of meaning detached from everyday life, and endowed with a peculiar reality of their own. Within the symbolic universe these detached realms of reality are integrated within a meaningful totality that 'explains,' perhaps also justifies them ... The symbolic universe is, of course, constructed by means of social objectivations. Yet its meaning-bestowing capacity far exceeds the domain of social life, so that the individual may 'locate' himself in it even in his most solitary experiences. (Berger and Luckmann 1966, 96)

I found that my clients wanted to locate themselves in a way that was independent of someone else's definition. This desire was characterized in the private and symbolic self-understanding that they developed within the broader social symbolism of language and human interaction in which they were engaged. Their multiple layers of self-developing awareness and the restoration of their 'subjugated knowledges' unfolded in what Berger and Luckmann called a 'symbolic universe' (1966, 96).

The 'meaning-bestowing capacity' to which Berger and Luckmann refer sometimes arises for my clients out of their dreams and forms the basis for an extemporaneous flood of insights. This development and its invaluable representation of ideas and experiences in therapy resemble what Mary Douglas describes as symbolic enactment. She argues that symbols 'can permit knowledge of what would otherwise not be known at all. [They do] not merely externalize experience, bringing it out into the light of day, but ... modif[y] experience in so expressing it' (1966, 64). What is perhaps Douglas's most important point, as it relates to my own findings, is her conclusion that 'it is very possible to know something and then find words for it' (62). This statement supplies the essence of the importance of symbolism, with which the women I present have grappled. The symbol often arrives first, and it is only later interpreted within the therapeutic dialogue. Here, too, lies a sensitive dimension of the explicative and reflexive aspect of therapy. Some symbols must remain undeciphered, and therefore private, so as not to destroy the essence of their message or risk trivializing the client's experience. Others demand translation. In any event, those symbols, some deciphered and others simply shared, create a place of mutual understanding and common meaning.

From Therapeutic to Social Research: A Reciprocal Substantiation

The subjective and often symbolic work of the reflexive therapeutic approach has much to offer to social and cultural theorists who are interested in that threshold between the intimate and the mostly unrecorded experiences of therapy and the well-documented social world to which my clients seek to return. Yet this potential source of insight was not commonly accessible to sociological analysis in such an immediate and direct way. It struck me early in my transition to the discipline of sociology that my position as therapist shared many features of social science's participant observer.

My clients' stories offered a body of knowledge based on substantive fieldwork from which theories on the distinction and interrelationship of private and public spaces could be further analysed. As testimony to and evidence of important personal events, these accounts revealed, sometimes with diary-like intimacy, the widespread and abhorrent social practice of forced and/or coerced sexual intercourse and other varieties of sexual exploitation of girls and women. How these acts affected their victims was, of course, central to my former role as a therapist. Each of these narratives or accounts was also a form of communication that inwardly reconnected the narrators' disparate parts of themselves, and, in due course, reconstructed and returned that self to a social world. For each woman, her account therefore helped to realign her with a socially shared but also socially constructed view of who she was.

This subjective work that occurred during the reconstruction of the client's account, especially before it was made public, is an area that has been little discussed in sociology. And yet these early stages of narrative formation reveal a process that is as much social as it is intrapersonal. In light of this discovery, I became interested in how account content is formed, as well as what each telling reveals or conceals. The culture that purports to describe the client's personal experience is ever present in the private dialogue with self as the client searches for an authentic and unique analysis of the abuse that has so transformed her life. Clifford Geertz describes this cultural presence, where it interferes and renders us unstable, as a form of haunting (1983, 9), for at the public level, the anticipated social reception of these accounts has a weighty influence on the shaping of the client's account and, I have also found, the public role can stifle the accounts' capacity for serving as a medium of self-reparation.

The therapist within the reflexive therapeutic process acts as a mediator between a client's individual revelations and external definitions of what these experiences of abuse signify. On the one hand, my clients' narratives represented an avenue of negotiating the 'how to' of self-construction and of social construction, linking private and public worlds. On the other hand, significantly, these close analyses extended beyond the immediate context of therapy. They illustrate how, for example, socially constructed meaning emerges. As such, these accounts had a more universal quality. In her work on vernacular risk perception Diane Goldstein succinctly underscores the merit of examining the kind of particularized, intimate, and local work such as evolves from our therapeutic negotiations. 'Meaning,' she says, 'is situated and emergent' (2004, 35). In their unfolding, narratives facilitate a deeper understanding of the nature and impact of such experiences and they represent vital therapeutic resources. The significance of these close analyses reverberate well beyond their therapeutic value, in showing how, for example, meaning emerges more generally, yet these narratives also hold interest and merit in themselves.

In some respects, my clients' accounts perform a social function similar to the historic role of the criminal confession, as 'acts of communication which confirmed the existence of a shared ethical view and a common human nature' (Hepworth and Turner 1982, 151). Like the subjects of Hepworth and Turner's study, my clients had existed on the social margins and then similarly found themselves in the public eye as never before. They offered a unique perspective on 'the dark corners' of our society made tangible through vernacular expression – their own form of confession. In turn, these secular confessions helped to relocate a common humanity.

My work on these clients' accounts reinforces Dorothy Smith's (1987) argument for the necessity of conducting research from inside the situation. The complex interpersonal dynamics in my relationship with my clients demanded the proximity that Smith's approach not only considers, but indeed honours. Certainly, at the therapeutic level, it is vital to interpret the client's experience from inside her immediate world. This is where she functions and has invited me to be. Such a level of closeness in research also provides analytical advantages. The alternative, a more detached scientific mode of research, as non-participant observer, would exclude the observer from the observed in the name of 'objectivity,' and the subject would be left on the 'other side' of the observer. Within this framework, the client is treated as if immune to the effects of external observation. Not only does this approach position the observer above and beyond the subject, but such a placement is undesirable, if not also impossible, within the context of my therapeutic approach. For the observer it also risks being denied access to the subject's inner world.

Smith's words best illustrate my insider's position, as therapist and as researcher. 'Like Jonah, the observer is inside the whale' (1987, 142). Smith uses this splendid biblical metaphor to encapsulate the essence and the inescapability of being inside another's experience as the researcher is in the midst of her work. I have been immersed in the unique experiences of another, and I would also have become, in fact, ineffective as a therapist if I had attempted to apply recipe solutions or distance myself too greatly from my client's reality. Smith's symbolic placement of the observer and observed together inside the belly of the beast reflects perfectly my own unique sense of place, as both therapist and researcher, in both sharing the client's context and wanting to reliably convey the significance of her account from her vantage point. Significantly, Smith does not see this positioning of the sociological enquirer – of being inside the subject's experience – as requiring a self-conscious adjustment or manipulation, since, in her view, inside is where we most comfortably locate ourselves anyway.

Yet while I intersect with Smith (1987) on the matter of standpoint, our intersection is approached from different directions. Smith arrives at the immediate or local vantage point by first considering the relations of ruling, mediated by documents and texts, and the forms of organization that constitute them. In contrast I most often begin with a client's immediate context – her words, her silences – and, in a reflexive dialogue, expand our interpretation outwards to consider her perception of herself by looking from the outside in.

Researching sexual abuse from the perspective of another discipline and grappling with the different set of questions that accompany this shift has transformed my original questions and produced new ones. A sociological perspective has allowed me to couple critical inquiry and intellectual scepticism with the empathy and compassion elicited in my capacity as therapist. This sociological vantage point has provided me with additional means for tracking ideas outside my first field, and it has given me an outlet for thinking critically without prematurely challenging the sometimes tentative and budding reconstructions of my clients. But perhaps foremost, my sociological inquiry into this private process has heightened my consciousness of the integral links between the intrapersonal experiences of my clients and their social worlds.

Nikolas Rose directs us to the legitimacy and the value of the forms of self-reconstruction in which my clients were engaged. 'To speak of the invention of the self is not to suggest that we are, in some way, the victims of a collective fiction or delusion. That which is invented is not an illusion; it constitutes our truth' (1996, 3). Here Rose exposes the fissures between private and social perceptions of selfhood, but also locates the importance of hearing private accounts and of admitting them into social research. Similar insights on authenticity and self-construction have been reached by many former clients, each in her fashion. Ultimately, their embodied, local reality stands as validity enough for them. Somewhat ironically, once clients have rejected the social and traditional therapeutic pressures to make their accounts conform to what are supposedly more universal and objective standards and methods of truth, but ones that did not naturally fit them, their stories reflect more authentically their experience.

The Accounts

The initial chapter of this study describes and discusses the therapeutic and sociological influences on my practice and research. What follows next are the detailed accounts of representative clients. Each of chapters 3 through 6 contains a single narrative that marks the different stages of their collective reparation. In general the arrangement mirrors the client's presentation of herself in therapy. First the client begins by presenting her story from a perspective somewhere outside of herself, as if she were an outsider looking in. This perspective reflects the separation of body from self that most of my clients describe as a result of experiencing sexual exploitations. The distance from her account and her disembodiment combine to create for her an emotional divergence from her own story that, while at first necessary, must eventually be reconciled. The next stage is marked by the client's intimate and emotionally charged telling of her narrative. Subjective and intrapersonal analytical work that then follows grants the client a sense of realignment. Finally, as the therapeutic process concludes, the client's gaze broadens once again to encompass her view of herself as embodied and social.

The initial stage of therapy, as reflected in a client's story, is discussed in some detail in chapter 2, 'Locating the Self: The Language of Survival.' As the reader will see, my enquiry into the nature of the 'survivor' has led down several roads. The often-used, even hackneyed term *survival* has been almost inextricably linked to the subject of sexual abuse. It is a far-reaching social construction that attempts to describe and then to categorize an individual's capacity for surmounting an ordeal, a symbolic death in life, and, sometimes literally, a near death. But, though there are benefits to such objectification, the drawbacks of incorporating this term into the client's self-description and self-concept are also multiple and problematic. Not the least of these shortcomings has been how the expression *survivor* has altered my client's perception of her private experience, in its inherent insistence on a connection to a wider group of similarly traumatized people, and in their pursuit of a technique for recovery. The client's relationship to such descriptions represents an important part of her altering self-concept. It is generally her desire to be typical and not to stand alone, as most of have had to do secretly for many years. This desire usually results in an initial adoption of such commonly used descriptions as *survivor*. Later, however, my clients typically recognize that such categorizations are limiting, so they begin to reshape those external identities imposed by the dominant culture. This chapter, then, examines in detail how externally manufactured language and definitions have defined my client's experiences and self-perception.

Chapter 3, 'Anguish, Dreams, and Remembering: The Reflexive Process,' allows the reader entry into a further dimension of my client's private and subjective world of personal reconstruction. It is in this phase of therapy that the client begins anew her search for effective personal and creative remedies to alleviate her sense of alienation. Dreams and the metaphors they offer are now often actively employed to bring this feat to fruition. This chapter looks specifically at reflexivity as the essential process that underscores the narrative and fuels her work on her own reconstruction. For the client, until a personal symbol has been spoken, it represents meaning that has been unmanipulated from without. However, in searching for understanding and validation, she seeks to share her thoughts and imagery. Her reflexive processes begin to dominate, as the therapist and client interpret and reinterpret personal symbolism. These creative acts supplant the stagnation of a fixed description, such as 'victim' or 'survivor,' with something more powerful, self-sustaining, and essentially personal in her search for reintegration. The rewards springing from a reflexive inquiry eventually motivate the client to dispense with an objectified, static, and ultimately ineffective 'solution' to her problems borrowed from an external source.

Chapter 4, 'From Silence to Narration: Exposing and Interpreting a Fragmented Self,' elucidates the next stage in the client's transition from her private reworking of self to the public presentation of that 'new' self. This chapter centres on the experience of account formation and expression, and how and why each client constructs and relays her reconstructed narrative. In understanding more fully what happens, we examine the sources that she draws upon for the substance and sustenance of this self-redefinition. The personal and social significance of each revision, as well as the transformations that occur within her through the telling, first made me conscious of the patterns common to individual narratives and evokes their collective significance.

Of course whether or not a client's story is believed, or whether there occurs a positive and/or negative reception once it is expressed, necessarily influences my clients' concepts of themselves. Chapter 5, 'Private Worlds, Public Worlds, and the Pursuit of Certainty,' explores the account form, its public reception, and the accompanying private and public pursuit of certainty. There is a fragile relationship between respecting and honouring the unique qualities of each account and searching for the common links between the individual story and others. This fissure between subjective and objective meaning leads us to consider the matter of 'truth' in account formation, especially from my clients' perspective. In turn, truth and associated issues of credibility and ambiguity have forced me to consider 'the cultural grid of intelligibility' (Kogan and Brown 1998, 497), or where my clients' stories, as sexual-abuse narratives, fit into a wider social pattern of acceptance or non-acceptance. Some questions explored in this vein include how the client and therapist can accept, as legitimate, memories that are mere fragments when there are strong public pressures to dismiss them as fabrications or false memories. In addition, I look at how each client deals with her own lack of surety, as her subjective account sometimes collides with a dominant cultural narrative. This chapter therefore represents a point of intersection between the client and me, and a point of departure, as her going public allows me to introduce these narratives for scrutiny by a wider therapeutic and sociological audience.

Each chapter therefore explores a different dimension of the recreation and hence reparation of self, as viewed through a slightly different lens. Ultimately the individual chapters combine to offer the reader a range of reflections upon an interconnected, multilayered experience that integrates the intrapersonal with the public self. Collectively, they reveal the client's evolving self-description, as it broadens to encompass an external view of her. For in reinventing and subsequently repairing the self, her identity is inextricably bound to a wider social and cultural identity, and what she has experienced is again defined in social and cultural terms.

More importantly, successful therapy cannot proceed by merely treating the symptoms or the individual in isolation. It is central that the reconstructed self re-establish and measure itself within a wider social framework. This position is affirmed by certain symbolic interactionists and feminist scholars (Shearer-Cremean and Winkelmann 2004). Moreover, it is not the 'survivor' who holds the 'truth.' Nor is it the therapist. Rather an understanding of what has happened to the client is a negotiated one even better understood through the prism of social research. My task is to discuss and compare social and therapeutic descriptions of self, and to explore the results of my own twofold pursuit, as therapist and researcher, as it has been shaped by my clients' accounts.

Finally, it should be noted that there are limits to sociological knowledge and inquiry as it pertains to the therapeutic. No participant observer, as sociologist alone, enters the intimate and the personal as intimately as a therapist who is trusted by the client, who is entrusted with her account, and who engages with the client in this fascinating delving into the self. This work has forged an interchange between the internal and external perspectives and the two disciplines that allows others to step close to these inner, intimate worlds and thus discern the significant sociological benefits of doing so.

1 A Sociologist/Therapist's View 'from inside the Whale'

The therapeutic approach I developed over time is best summarized as a reflexive, feminist, and interpretative style that cultivated symbolic understanding and narrative expression. A mutual scrutiny of the narrative brought to light dominant social and cultural ideologies. The diverse nature of this process grew out of our combined efforts to understand the many levels of my clients' fragmented selves, and eventually it yielded an effective therapeutic model. I began this therapeutic project from the grounded perspective of my clients' accounts and worked outwards, inductively. In so doing, I continuously reviewed and modified my therapeutic skills to enable the narratives of my clients to unfold, not the other way around. In this sense, my applied theoretical orientation became a product of negotiation from within a therapeutic alliance.

Central for each client was her own account reconstruction. In developing their narrated reintegration of self, most clients tended to create or locate symbols and/or metaphors quite independently of the therapist. Such processes brought them closer to an original self-perception of what had happened to them and distanced them from the dominant cultural description of their abuse. In tracking this phenomenon, I explore the social impediments to clients' efforts towards self-definition and study the avenues that best illuminate their attempts at reparation. In my dual role as sociological participant observer and therapist, I present in the following study the processes through which my clients' accounts, as they expressed them, became negotiated, articulated, and transcribed.

This chapter demonstrates how sociology and related social research have informed my understanding and broader predilection to investigate narrative's self-defining capacities, and how this focus, in turn, enabled my two professional interests, sociology and therapy, to intersect. I thus reach beyond the scope of the therapeutic to integrate the significance of the social role in the reinterpretation and reshaping of women's sexual exploitation accounts. This analysis also extends to consider other social research that, by virtue of its emphasis on subjective dimensions of personal experience, establishes nascent associations between therapeutic and social science discourses. The sociological and therapeutic methods and research that I draw together here have assisted my intellectual mediation of the two disciplines by providing commonality. I delineate below how my therapeutic and sociological approaches have dovetailed in an exploration of how the social affects personal meaning-making following sexual trauma. Traditionally analytical therapy has stressed the intrapersonal dimension of self-transformation, while sociology has focused on the collective aspect of such change. My interest, as a practising therapist and a professional sociologist, is to study and understand that region between the intrapersonal and larger social experience of self. In order to describe and analyse my clients' projects of reparation, therefore, I integrate a range of scholarship on embodiment, trust, the objectification of women's experiences, the reflexive role of social forces in the shaping of the private self, and the socially bridging and restorative properties of the private narrative, to mention some. This literature explains clients' attempts to make sense of and merge their reintegrated selves back into their peopled worlds. It also is a conceptual basis for the intra- and interpersonal exchanges that define the therapeutic dialogue and its sociological context. Each perspective discussed centres, sometimes only indirectly, on a distinct aspect of reflexive identity re/formation. Yet no single theory has comprehensively managed to describe this reintegration process.

The accounts that surfaced in my clients' therapeutic work were attempts to understand and integrate an experience that had left them alienated from their families, their wider social networks, and most notably from themselves. While these women did not all consciously enter therapy to reconstruct their stories, the vast majority of them strongly attempted to do just that. In the course of giving expression to and hence re-envisioning their previously unspoken experiences, many clients implicitly came to realize what Holocaust survivor Elie Wiesel has stated so well: 'The unspeakable draws its force and its mystery from its own silence' (1990, 165). Speaking out helps to eradicate the power of the unspeakable and demystify the client's silence.

Reflexivity: Private and Social

Reflexiveness is a common thread that permeates each account represented here and links together my therapeutic and sociological research. Reflexivity, that dialectical exchange and negotiation of meaning, of researching and reinterpretation, sits at the centre of each new narrative and continuously transforms the perspectives of client, therapist, and researcher alike. This continuously evolving understanding, aptly described by Myerhoff as a 'consciousness about being conscious; thinking about thinking,' underscores each client's account and renders each telling, a significantly reconstructive and potentially unique experience (1992, 307). Properly facilitated, this understanding connects the subjective inner workings of the personal narrative to the wider social environment.

In general, my clients readily integrated the reflections of their narrative produced by our exchanges into their new constructions. Feedback on their intrapersonal plight is exactly what they sought. Self-reflection and therapeutic reflexiveness enabled them to see themselves, sometimes for the first time, and fostered a potential for asserting their own identity in their new role as creators. My assisting them to locate such a new-found self-reliance and encouraging them to listen to their own authority marked an early stage of a clearly wider, reflexive process. Further along the reflexive loop, the internalization of the client's newly cultivated symbols helped her to interpret and construct a new self, a reinvention she willingly shared in our therapeutic exchange. In this process, her sense of autonomy and her conviction of personal agency were restored and enhanced.

It was however nearly impossible for my clients, victimized most often by adult men who were or remained in an authoritative and trusting relationship, to return to their former and habitual acceptance of traditional authorities. Nevertheless, they sought a healing that was as much social as intrapersonal. Consequently, they became engaged in a reflexive re-examination of themselves and, necessarily, of their unique relationship to their social environment, in order to come to terms with such fundamental interpersonal and social cornerstones as trust, and to revisit the disembeddedness of traditional authority in their own lives.

In seeking to reconcile this lost trust and to overcome their disillusionment with authority, they externalized their experiences of sexual assault through their narratives by using internal and external symbols and metaphors. This mechanism of re-adaptation, which my clients directed but to which our therapeutic ritual lent support, entailed a reflexive remapping of their individual life stories. It also typically involved the client's identification and reclamation of inner authority to replace the failure of external authorities, and a casting off of ill-fitted symbols of the traditional system that they saw as having manipulated or failed them. This reconstruction that often integrated rituals, symbols, and/or metaphors of the clients' making, encapsulated and made accessible their otherwise inexpressible experiences. This reconstituted self, in turn, fostered self-trust and embodied a reconstituted inner authority – the cornerstones of recovery.

As a participant in my clients' reflexive projects, I became caught up in their individual quests while also contributing to them a broad social, cultural, and contextual understanding of sexual-abuse narratives. I, as Smith maintains, operated within a shared textually mediated discourse under similar relations of ruling. I was a product of a wider community that prepared me to hear such stories, I worked from within the account of the sexually violated client, and I evolved alongside her, as she prepared herself to reconstruct her story. In this sense, it became a mutually informed pursuit. In this explicit form, reflexivity became a thread common to both of our missions and a reflexive transformation began to take shape within our specific therapeutic context.

Narrative and identity formation are closely linked subjects in sociological and therapeutic literature. In analysing their current usage in the social sciences, Jane Elliot attributes our heightened interest in reflexivity to a change in the way we view ourselves. She also says, 'The notion of identity as a reflexive achievement emphasizes the autonomy of individuals in making choices and shaping their own lives.' This she terms the 'reflexive modernization thesis' and explains it as 'the argument that identity is now both increasingly flexible and individualized' (2005, 153). It is therefore no mere coincidence that I and other theorists/practitioners emphasize reflexivity in our work.

Myerhoff has shed unique light on reflexivity and the project of 're-authoring of self' in 'Life Not Death in Venice,' where she captures the importance of performance to the regeneration of meaning. Her focus, unlike my own, was on a more deliberate and contrived performance, as a way to unearth hidden aspects of peoples' biographies, but she also touched directly on the role of the creative self and the 'inner world' (1992, 267). In this anthropological study of a seniors centre in southern California with a predominately elderly Jewish membership, she details a collective act of self-definition through a reflective process, as a marginalized group of Holocaust survivors painted, wrote about, and performed their past onstage in an assertion of their identity. By such means, they actualized formerly invisible lives or knowledge of past experiences that had become subjugated. By loudly repudiating their invisibility, isolation, and impotence, they made themselves seen and heard. In making themselves seen, they also came into being but on their own terms, in re-authoring themselves (263).

This theme of self-authorship and resistance to repudiation is directly significant in my clients' work. They created their own self-definition through dream analysis, journal writing, construction of art forms, and telling of metaphorically laden and representative stories. The meaning inherent in their accounts was, like those of Myerhoff's subjects, made richer through the act of performance; it contributed to self-definition as well as to self-reparation. In their own spontaneous portrayals of self, they affected a result similar to those of Myerhoff's participants. They too created a kind of mirror that reflected their own experience back to them. In other ways too the 'definitional ceremonies' acted out by Myerhoff's subjects were similar to my clients' meaning-making. A marked similarity is also found in the results. Myerhoff contends that the externalization of personally selected symbolic representations of ourselves, for the purpose of self- and external validation, produced a 'profoundly reflexive occasion ... which gives human experience its second life' (269). It was this second life that I saw in my clients. They did so by enacting those parts of themselves or of those moments in their history that symbolized their marginalized selves. In Myerhoff's analysis, the seniors' ceremony represented 'their rejection of the assigned position of helpless victims' (269). Just as this act permitted Myerhoff's population to enact their 'vision' and cast off their feelings of stigmatization, so it did with my clientele.

Like Myerhoff's subjects, the women I present in the following chapters are engaged in a vital and intricate social exchange that promotes self-awareness through an intellectual and emotional integration of terrible experiences. Yet, like Myerhoff's group, they recognize that self-awareness is impossible and the horrible events of the past are not 'bearable' until they have been assimilated into 'a form that endows meaning (266). Myerhoff unwittingly speaks to the experience of my sexually exploited clientele in the following passage:

When both the outside and the inner world deprive us of reflections – evidence that, indeed, we are still present and alive, seen and responded to – the threat to self-awareness can be great. Definitional ceremonies deal with the problem of invisibility and marginality; they are strategies that provide opportunities for being seen and in one's own terms, garnering witnesses to one's worth, vitality, and being. (1992, 267)

Myerhoff's subjects collectively brought about the self-redefinition that my clients sought through an intrapersonal location and integration of metaphors, and what they share was the recognition that symbolic representations of themselves are authentic and valuable. They also shared the desire to have these newly unearthed aspects of their accounts reflected back to them so that they saw them subjectively, thus fuelling additional insights. Through my clients' accounts, as revealed in dreams and significant memories, they came to understand and express what external labels simply could not provide. The textually mediated discourse on sexual abuse that purported to describe their experiences and the mainstream representation of sexual abuse in such terms as *victim* and *survivor* could not achieve for my clients what their own symbolically rendered descriptions did.

Our identity is the sum total of our self-awareness. Key to this notion is that self-identity is flexible but not completely malleable. Thus self-identity becomes a reflexive project that we continuously work and reflect upon. We incessantly revise and adjust each account, the story of who we are and how we came to be where we are now (Giddens 1991, 53). This analysis supports my therapeutic findings that clients' identities are never complete. Nor can they simply and spontaneously be changed. They are fluid yet interconnected, as Anthony Giddens argues. But importantly, this interconnection renders them more stable, because, as revealed in our therapeutic exchanges, reflexive transformation is essential to the ascription of personal meaning and the creation of a shared understanding among family members and the wider community, even the global one.

Such concerns with micro- and macro-levels of reflexivity, as interconnected – an interest pursued much earlier by Georg Simmel in 'The Stranger' (1971) – extends to sociology, which seeks to illuminate intrapersonal territories and tie them to social ones. It also has necessary carryover into the social dimension of the therapeutic experience. In contrast to the approach of Giddens, however, we must work from the inside outwards.

Social Research Perspectives on Personal Account Construction

I have come to realize and appreciate more profoundly that the yearning to tell and to be understood is rooted in my clients' need for a healing that is intrapersonal, but also social. Like the confession, reflexive therapy is a self-regulating and self-defining practice that connects us to others. Rose writes, 'In confessing, one is subjectified by another, for one confesses in the actual or imagined presence of a figure who prescribes the form of the' confession, the words and rituals through which it should be made, who appreciates, judges, consoles, or understands. But in confessing, one also constitutes oneself' (1989, 240). This viewpoint recognizes the socially reflexive nature of the therapeutic 'confession' while upholding its significance as a pathway to self-definition.

While most clients begin their therapeutic account with a predetermined audience – the therapist – with the intention of terminating their silence, from there the route is not so direct. Giving voice to the 'unspeakable' cannot be a lone act. There is a need for private, secular 'confessions,' insofar as they play a role in the personal reconstruction, but the relationship to the 'confessor,' to the therapist in this context, is not straightforward. The 'confessor' that my clients sought was not neutral but an engaged intermediary between their intrapersonal experiences and their social worlds. As a therapist I acted to some extent as a conduit for externalizing their pain. They may have initiated the therapeutic relationship to seek, as Foucault contends, validation through confession, but the legitimization they eventually reconciled themselves to was a negotiated one that honoured both internal and external participation (1980a, 66).

The 'confession' typically returns the client to a selected point in her autobiography, from where she begins to revise her experience in words other than those socially prescribed, and in a form only she is capable of making bearable. Confessional details vary greatly from one client's example of sexual exploitation to another, such as the age of onset, the social and cultural environment in which these events took place, the extent of the associated violence, and the frequency and duration of abuse. Distinct too was each woman's level of identification with the nature of her exploitation and her reasons for ultimately relating her narrative to someone else.

Most clients quite independently created or located symbols and/or metaphors during the course of therapeutic analysis and throughout the process of their storied reintegration of self. I encouraged these efforts, as they brought them closer to an original self-perception while simultaneously distancing them from the dominant cultural description of their abuse. Each narrative production during therapy allowed the client and therapist to search collaboratively for new meanings, which facilitated a deeper general and mutual understanding of the sexual-abuse account. Central to my therapeutic work, therefore, was the question of how each client reconstructed her own account. Out of this process that was unique for each client there materialized an original and individual approach to relaying these accounts.

The how and the why of an account's social reception is problematic, yet significant. To begin, the private story cannot be received until the public is ready to hear it. The most external dimension of the client's reflexive reparation – the public – is remote from her immediate and intimate world, yet closely tied to her own reflexive process and necessary in producing (or not) a climate that is right for the telling. In this regard, Ken Plummer suggests that a 'voice with no listener is a silence' (1995, 25). 'Stories', he also argues, 'can be told when they can be heard' (120). In other words, he contends that the two agents, the individual and the common, have to be more or less synchronous, if the story is to be received.

The Russian nesting doll is an appropriate analogy for describing the multilayered and reflexive unfolding of my clients' stories. Each layer, from the intrapersonal to the social, is contained one within the next and therefore dependent upon the others' unveiling and reception. Like the assembly of the nesting doll, the telling of the story needs to follow an individually determined sequence in order for it to surface and flourish. In short, the timing and form of the story's disclosure must conform to a certain pattern of social receptivity.

How is this social climate that is so necessary to the story's reception created? To some extent, the discourse on sexual abuse that has emerged only in the past generation follows Foucault's (1972) schema of discursive formation. Where the subject of women's sexual abuse was once hidden, it emerged and then came to exist within a field of discourse. It evolved to embody discussion, literature, and therapeutic practice. This particular discursive formation can also be related to a series of historical events: the rise of the feminist critique, the public issue of violence against women and post-traumatic stress syndromes among Holocaust survivors and veterans, the 'discovery' of child sexual abuse, the emergence of feminist therapy, and postmodernism. It can be understood, as Foucault suggests, as 'a fragment of history, a unity and discontinuity in history itself, posing the problem of its own limits, its divisions, its transformations, the specific modes of its temporality rather than its sudden irruption in the midst of the complicities of time' (1972, 117).

In further illuminating the emergence of this social climate, Nikolas Rose (1996) sees the issue of our social preparedness to accept a particular discourse, like sexual abuse, as happening in the following way. He offers a constructionist perspective and refers to the construction of persons as an assemblage of connections and linkages, of particular spaces and places. He argues that our social worlds are intimately interconnected and constructed. Thus a social motivation to hear sexual-abuse accounts does not happen without there being first a collective and historical preparedness. It is within such discourses and assemblages referred to by Foucault and Rose that the individual's private preparedness to voice her account of sexual exploitation rests and in which the therapist's openness, willingness, and formal preparation receives it.

After the initial confession, the therapist and the client together begin a co-facilitation of the account in which the therapist begins to participate more directly in the process of self-reconstruction. Here, my clients try to reverse – and to a certain extent succeed – the pre-existing social will to define them and its refusal to hear them, except on its own terms. Only then, as I've suggested, the client searches beyond the available constructions and discourses that have defined her experience to find a unique symbolism and self-description and, then, to incorporate herself within this new self-definition, first as its author, and consequently as its expert.

My clients in particular, and many women in general, are commonly unable to assert control over the gendered forces that dictate their existence, because they often lack personal authority and a capacity for self-expression. 'Over a lifetime and in the daily routines,' Smith writes, 'women's lives tend to show a loose, episodic structure that reflects the ways in which their lives are organized and determined external to them and the situations they order and control' (1987, 66–7). Such a lack of command over their daily lives, a feature shared by many of my clients, leaves them with the feeling that they are in the words of my client Jesse 'ricocheting out of control.' This, in turn, renders them especially vulnerable to a gender-based manipulation and exploitation. My professional experience of therapy with women supports Smith's notion that this is how women's lives unfold. Here too is the local level from which their insight and authority can spring and, as my clients have discovered, where the project of the re-authorship of the self must and does take form.

In this sense, Smith points to the necessity of focusing on the local, as opposed to the conceptual and extra-local, in making a sociology that is of and for women. In her exploration of women's relationships within, and their relationships to, their 'everyday world,' Smith indirectly emphasizes the importance of my own very immediate work with women's account formations. Although Smith does not stray far from the conscious realm to consider alternative levels of consciousness or meaning, she does uphold the importance of symbolism created by women. Smith's findings further apply to my own professional repositioning from practitioner to researcher, and then back again, particularly where she outlines a sociological approach that calls for the researcher to heighten her own consciousness about the impact of the experiences in which she participates, as well as the importance of transforming these into text.

> It means attending to the primary materiality of the text as an essential moment in the transition from the locally embodied to the discursive. Hence, in exploring how sociology is assembled and organized as actual practices in which we too participate and by which our practices too are organized, we are also engaged in a reflexive examination and critique of what we know how to do and do. (Smith 1999, 49)

Smith also highlights the reflexive nature of the transcription of experiences from the local world to the written text as an important acknowledgement of what is an onerous and mostly unseen process. She contends, and I agree, that this shift involves 'working from that site of knowing that is prior to the differentiation of subjective and objective' (1999, 49). It is one that demands that the transcriber be conscious of the subtleties and nuances of lived experience in order to spare her the fate of becoming objectified as discourse, for so much of what belongs to the client can be misrepresented, overlooked, or lost within that shift between private and social worlds. Authentic research, for Smith, derives from the equal treatment of these realms. Her contention that subjective and objective perspectives should not be separated is one that supports my contention of a connection of the intrapersonal world of therapy with the work of sociology and underscores the reflexivity of this endeavour.

   Smith's linkage accomplishes something else too. Smith believes that we, as feminist researchers, ought to operate from inside another's lifescape. This strategy makes room for the complicated interpersonal dimensions in my relationship with my clients that demand our ongoing revision. Given the therapeutic encouragement of the client to draw from her own resources, it becomes necessary to interpret her experiences from inside them. In refusing to prioritize the client's subjective and objective states, the therapeutic environment nurtures self-expression from inner sources that we would otherwise rarely give credence to, let alone view. Only this approach can do justice to the creative and often subjective foundations from which these clients' stories originate. It is necessary that these stories, which I carry over into my research, are examined with the same closeness.

Yet this immediacy of representation that these stories bring forth does not alone solve the problem (as Smith noted and I also regularly witness): a woman's isolation from her own experience. For if my client who as a result of her abuse or as a result of other social conditions is acquiescent about having her experiences interpreted for her, she beholds herself largely through the eyes of her therapist. This potential therapeutic manipulation of a client's relationship can render her, as Smith says, merely 'an object to herself' (1999, 30), and thereby undermine further her personal sense of validity. It is crucial therefore that the therapist keep the client's context continuously in mind, remaining ever vigilant about overpowering her tentative or budding attempts to express herself, in order that she can stand free from objectification and/or consummation by another's version of reality. In short, Smith's work is important for illuminating the marginalized position of women and in suggesting how a rethinking of sociological method can represent their unique and under-represented position in sociological literature and in society.

Complexities of Narrative Transcription

The therapeutic relationship, like the research relationship, is not static, with each party rigidly adhering to a defined role. Nor, aside from respecting ethical boundaries, does each client remain at a consistent or predictable emotional distance. The dynamic that is forged within this relationship between therapist and client is continuously undergoing examination and adjustment on both sides. The relationship adjusts itself to the content of the account as it is unearthed, as well as to what is not unearthed, and continuously transforms conscious and symbolic roles and expectations that are formed there. The flux of this relationship generates new meaning for both parties who are engaged in this evolving and reflexive interpretative exchange.

My presence in my clients' remaking was a concern to me. The therapist's appropriate distance from the client and the client's account was an issue with which I initially grappled in my capacity as therapist. I wondered to what extent I represented yet another discursive agent attempting to define her. As my understanding of clients' reconstructions developed, I came to realize that all narratives and hence all narrative therapy and research involves co-constructions (see Elliot 2005). None stand completely apart from social influences.

This threshold between defining and being defined represents one of the most complex dimensions of identity reconstruction in therapy. I eventually concluded that the ethical therapist, and indeed the researcher, needs to be most concerned about deliberately or inadvertently distorting the client's story through over-direction or by imposing personal projections upon a narrative that is not hers to direct. In short, therapist and researcher both need to remain ever conscious and respectful of their place in the narrative's unfolding and need to resist this urge to tidy things up. If the issues concerning roles and boundaries that then arise in the therapeutic encounter and punctuate the very nature of participant observation are rendered transparent, they can be cultivated advantageously within the therapeutic dialogue. Such clarification of positions promotes an exchange between the client and the therapist in which participants become freer to probe deeper meanings, such as the presence of multiple truths and validities.

Also a therapist's transcription of a client's story poses concerns about the potential alteration or subterfuge of meaning that can take place in the attempt to record the experiences of another, such as reflected in ethnographic research. Charles Lemert refers to the importance of 'not succumbing to the ethnographic romance – to the deep desire to find the true and real in order to tell a familiar story where everything turns out just as it should or must' (2002, 205). Nancy Hartstock isolates a further challenge confronting the social researcher, that sometimes, despite our best efforts or 'however well intentioned one may be, the real relations of humans with each other and with the natural world are not visible' (1987, 159). As intensive therapeutic work develops, for example, many levels of meaning are simultaneously negotiated. These factors and others combine to complicate each exchange enormously, and so too my communication of them to others. In short, there are always subtleties that are beyond our abilities to capture.

In light of such complexities, obviously none of the following narratives represents a clear, factual, untainted, and all-inclusive depiction of

the past. This is simply impossible to effect. As Batya Weinbaum concludes in her work on the language of sexual abuse in oral history, 'All
we really collect is an individual person's account of an event as rendered into a shared present, which in itself becomes yet another event'
(2004, 64). Weinbaum's research experience upholds personal accounts
as intangible, and yet she argues that this does not present an insurmountable problem. Despite her optimism, the perception of narratives
as impressionistic sources of meaning and, for that reason, as insub-
stantial or unreliable is widely held among researchers. A similar
demand for 'truth' or 'objectivity' plagues clients' expression and transmission of narratives. My clients, for example, face an ongoing tension
in their everyday lives over social credibility and personal validity
based on establishing 'the truth' of their experiences.

This tension created by the demand for objectivity that the women of
this study experience is also addressed by Shearer-Cremean and
Winkelmann. They maintain that 'the credibility of a narrative is determined by the receptivity of the audience' – an audience of which my
clients are acutely aware (2004, 19). The authors also argue that credibility can be reduced to the politics of language. These insights support
the idea that narrative reconstruction specifically, and therapy in general, cannot and must not be viewed in isolation from social and cultural influences. Many narrativists maintain, like Hinchman and
Hinchman, that 'stories are more than idiosyncratic or purely private
ruminations' and that they have 'transsubjective truth value,' yet this is
a perspective not always shared by those in my clients' social circles
(1997, xvi). I consider the position of truth in narrative more thoroughly in chapter 5. Suffice it to say here, that my clients and I deliberately dispense with any pursuit of absolute truth, or public receptivity,
in favour of concentrating on clients' assemblages of meaning.

A further and related social research challenge for me, as transcriber
of my clients' accounts, is likewise rooted in the problem of social perception. To the removed onlooker, these accounts do not have a neat or
predictable beginning, middle, or end. They were relayed selectivity by
my clients and thus have not evolved in a linear form. Because clients'
images and associated insights are often presented in a seemingly random fashion, this ostensibly arbitrary presentation, from the perspective of the outside audience, may detract from their credibility. Yet for
the narrator herself, there is often an internal logic and order of expression through which reflexive meaning is established (see Bruner 1987;

Elliot 2005; Hinchman and Hinchman 1997), which provides them with validation.

Clearly the perception of personal accounts from the outside looking in is a different one entirely from its perception from the inside out. That is why satisfying my clients' own sense of authenticity in the face of others' denial or disbelief of their abuse experience became an explicit purpose of their therapeutic journey. This focus, as Martin Kohli explains, is not to find an objective standard of truth, but rather one of the ways in which the narrative can inform the listener 'about how the subject thematizes and constructs his own biography (in a given situation) and, by doing this, reaffirms (or even constitutes) his identity, and plans his actions' (1981, 70). The significance of the account thus lies not in whether it supports the dominant cultural discourse on sexual abuse, but in its affirmative, transformative, and perhaps even protest value in what is an active and creative symbolic process.

Social Bodies / Private Bodies

One more persistent therapeutic and research concern in which social research has relatively recently engaged is to understand the complexities of clients' embodiment. The current sociological focus on embodiment, as a social manifestation, has helped in analysing the therapeutic narrative by contributing important social insights to what was previously considered the realm of the individual. It has historicized and politicized embodiment and, in so doing, has broadened the critique of what was otherwise perceived as a seemingly isolated and non-reflexive dimension of being. Bodies are a historical phenomenon, Rose claims, both in an individual and collective sense. They are 'thought bodies' or 'bodies of thought' (1996, 182–3). The body, in this sense, contains a collective awareness and knowledge.

My clients' experiences demonstrate that they are also more than mere forms of cognition, for they have undergone a holistic experience, the effects of which are strongly instilled in them but they do not necessarily understand or express. While their reaction to trauma and its related psychological distress was undoubtedly mediated by a social heritage linking the outer with the inner, it is also more than that. Theirs is an inexpressible violation of a multilayered self through a violation of the body. In their reparations they seek an understanding that is beyond the assemblages about which Rose speaks. For most of my clients, some form of disconnection from their bodies occurred as an outcome of their sexual exploitation. For that reason, the body became a salient concern in our therapeutic sessions. Because of their first-hand experience with disassociation and fragmentation, at the bodily level, my clients come to know, though not necessarily in analytical terms, that one area of the self cannot be fully understood in isolation from another.

In linking my clients' private experiences of embodiment to their account reconstructions, Burkitt's (1999) work on the sociology of the body and, in particular, his association of the body with a reality outside of language is important. He views symbols, like the body, as a dimension of reality that cannot be separated from space and time, and firmly classifies symbolic content, such as that frequently produced in my clients' reconstructive processes, as objective artefacts employed as forms of communication. He contends that such artefacts mediate relations at all levels, and argues,

> The symbolic deepens our understanding of, and our relationship to, the practical and embodied. The symbolic also makes possible the realm of imagination, or the imaginary, through which we attempt to understand the world in various ways. Through this medium we are connected to the world more deeply because we can attempt to understand it and our own actions within it in an imaginative way, and we can give meaning to the world that it does not have of, or within, itself. (Burkitt 1999, 84)

This perspective lends credence to the creative components of my clients' work of self-reparation by supporting, as legitimate and grounded, the dimension in which they are operating and seeking meaning. Their seemingly isolated and disembodied perspectives on their experience, that they re-envisage through symbol work, does not distance them from their reality, but connects them in meaningful ways. The work of producing personal symbols, through reflexivity, creates social meaning and, according to Burkitt, separates the 'active agents who make things happen' from the 'passive patients' who are the recipient or the reactors to the actions of others' (1999, 85). In this way, embodied symbolic productions empower the individual personally and socially. Initially it was usually too painful for the client to directly confront an intimate exploration of what the body had endured and the indignities associated with those violations. This would have necessitated that she look directly and candidly at the source of her shame – her formally appropriated and physically violated being. For this reason, at the client's direction, her body was usually attended to more obliquely, at first always through a metaphoric and/or symbolic perspective. Essentially, clients found it less threatening to work with and digest the issue of their embodiment if it was symbolically represented.

The individual cannot be fully conceived when separated from her social world, and exploring embodied responses to social invasions of the self highlights the many levels at which individuals respond to and are inseparable from wider social constructions. My clients' projects of redefinition separated them from the passivity manifested in their former state of victimization. Inextricably tied to symbolic reparations and grounded in the body, their newly defined identities were later projected outwards for affirmation, thus completing a cycle of reflexive transformation by means of their subsequent integration of social perceptions.

Interpretation and Use of Symbolism

Just as the body has been perceived as an unmanageable realm and previously all but ignored by sociology, so too has personal symbolism. Yet symbols and symbolic expression have held and continue to hold a place of prominence in my counselling work and in my sociological research. My clients' urge to redefine and to reposition themselves independently of others' representations of them was consistently characterized by a personal and symbolic effort to understand themselves. They located symbols and adapted them in order to encapsulate a sometimes unutterable experience. This content was first tried out in the therapeutic arena where the method of exchange itself was searching, open, and encouraging, and we used these internally rendered symbols as a tool for framing, ordering, heightening consciousness of, and communicating abuse experiences. In effect, analytical work with symbolism that therapist and client include in therapy underscored the source of many of my clients' reconstructive processes. This approach proved most often to be the best method of reaching into, understanding, and communicating experiences that were otherwise difficult to contain.

My own interest in symbolic expression was stimulated early on by the works of C.G. Jung and his interpretation of dreams. The Jungian approach provided important insights into women's symbolic, metaphoric, and literal relationships to their own embodiment. And it brought into sharp relief the extent to which, for many of my clients, their accounting process or narrative was a symbolic act of self-reparation. The specific dreams and examples of symbolic exchange gathered here were selected from this body of material and identified by each client as having contributed to significant and unexpected personal insights.

Discovering and appropriating the symbols integral to making unique each account helped individual clients to shape and define a new and often an innovative self-definition. This dream work demonstrated a fresh set of symbolic reference points, which were sometimes reached through a deliberate searching, but were most frequently produced spontaneously and/or unconsciously. This process proved crucial for those who were attempting to personalize, integrate, and communicate an experience of fragmentation that had identified and labelled them – one in which their self-understanding was neglected and one in which personal narrative and self-creation played only minor roles.

Denzin contends that instances of profound perception, as revealed in a dream or recollected image, are truly original and uninfluenced by all else, but they are brief and ephemeral. Moreover, as he puts it, 'We can never get back to raw biographical experience. The closest we can ever get is when a subject, in a moment of epiphany, moves from one social world to another. In these instances the subject is between interpretative frameworks. When this happens, experience is described in words that have not yet been contaminated by the cultural understandings of a new group' (1992, 91). In intensive therapeutic work, the culturally uncontaminated words expressed by the client are extracted from personally rendered metaphors, such as those produced in dreams. Precisely, this personal appropriation of metaphor makes the process unique and offers each client access to a non-prescribed language and meaning system. For when a client has retreated from the social world that has, in her view, alienated her through objectification, she inevitably becomes estranged from the language and symbolism associated with that world. The powerfully exploitative experience that has caused each client to withdraw from her social environment thus becomes also the catalyst for the development of a new framework of communication.

Sometimes the content evoked by a symbol or metaphor strikes a client with such intensity and subsequent sense of accuracy that her recognition of it leads to a 'magnified moment' – a term that Arlie Hochschild uses to reflect on moments of epiphany or unusual insight (1983, 4). Such an effect enables them to locate, trust, and adopt their own 'truths' in whatever form they have presented themselves in their dreams or the reframing of their reality that was often an expansion of dream analysis. In turn, their engagement with such personally rendered, transformative material gives them authority and further insight, because these moments affirm what the Jungian therapist and writer Marion Woodman describes as the role of the symbol. She writes, 'Jung believed that the healing was in the symbol, for the symbol brings together body, mind and soul through the creative imagination. The poet in touch with the collective unconscious is given the exact symbol which, when read, brings goose flesh to our bodies, meaning to our minds, and tears to our eyes. Momentarily we are one' (1982, 88–9). Just as a client's perception of disembodiment following sexual assault is symbolic, so too can her reconnection to those disparate parts of herself be achieved symbolically or metaphorically. In their process of comprehending what had been done to them, these women recognize and internalize the self-rendered words and symbols, their own constructions, that were encompassing and 'true' enough to reflect and represent their abusive experiences on the many levels at which they were affected.

Public Intercession in Private Constructions

Along independent lines of inquiry, Richard Sennett, Nikolas Rose, and Anthony Giddens ask us to consider reflexivity and the shaping of the private self. Their concerns lie with the powerful social and discursive forces that attempt to describe and define that self. These authors question the degree of freedom we actually have to control and create ourselves in light of such dominant and pervasive influences, and they describe the remodelling of the individual that they see occurring in the wake of a significant social shift and explore such issues as self reinvention and the role of the narrative in light of a certain social disintegration. In so doing, their arguments link my clients' private courses of account formation to public mediation of experience through the common thread of reflexivity.

In *The Corrosion of Character*, Sennett examines the way that self-identity is transformed at the personal level through insecurity generated in the workplace. He describes the attendant anxiety aroused by the change in expectations that occurs whenever rules are replaced by

strategies. In one line of inquiry, his study addresses the demise of loyalty among workers in loosely structured organizations. He concludes
that fragmented systems lead to a loss of trust, which at best 'invites reinvention and revision' (1998, 48). In this analysis Sennett's subjects,
like my clients, are essentially forced to remake themselves in the face
of great social insecurity. His study traces the effects of the disintegration of loyalty and trust from the collective experience down to the individual one. At issue for Sennett, as for my clients, is the void created
when trust is dissipated (142), and like his subjects, my clients are
engaged in a reflexive act that is analogous to a condition of 'moder-
nity/late modernity.'

Their experience as a displaced group lacking the 'inoculation' (Giddens 1991, 39) that trust provides, extends this important discourse in
an era when the relationship between the demise of private and public
trust has become, to quote Adam Seligman, 'conflictual' (1997, 99).
Once, public trust was seen to rest on private trust. This conflict poses a
significant social problem that the clients' private reworking of self
must address. I suggest that my clients' individual processes of re-
establishing trust, captured in their private and symbolic remaking,
represent a vital currency for social research, because their constructions at the micro-level suggest the tools necessary for rebuilding trust
in the face of its social erosion, described by Sennett and Seligman. A
sense of vulnerability and disorientation is commonly identified
among my clients as a result of a loss of trust and socially imposed
autonomy. Independence and autonomy – the solutions offered to the
workers of Sennett's study – are, however, inadequate substitutes for
trust either for his subjects or for my clients. Instead, they must locate
an intermediary stabilizing force to substitute for what is no longer
available to them. My clients eventually locate an internally rendered
and hence more stable source of trust and validity through their in-
depth and reconstructive therapeutic work.

Sennett is also interested in the social bridging and restorative properties of personal accounts in ascertaining the personal benefits that
emanate from a private reinvention of self. In this context, he suggests
that the people in his study 'attempted a kind of self healing' through
their narratives. What he ultimately saw as the greatest value of this
narrative process was its capacity to order their lives and, in so doing,
at least create an illusion of keeping randomness at bay. 'Narrative,' he
insightfully concludes, 'does the work of healing through its structure

... not through offering advice' (1998, 134). Among my clients, the creation or restoration of order was not the only benefit; equally important was a returning sense of certainty. My clients used the story milieu – much like the workers of Sennett's study – at times unconsciously and sometimes quite deliberately as an avenue for building into their lives a sense of continuity and a method of ordering past chaos.

At the onset of therapy, many of my clients felt there was no source upon which to reconstruct a narrative, because their past had been devastated by an atrocity that they did not wish to incorporate into their account. In other words, upon entering therapy, they often viewed their lives as a story of failure that they wished to obliterate rather than investigate. Most therefore initially placed little stock in the therapeutic benefits of conveying their narrative. Yet their consistent return to this means reflected an underlying belief, or hope perhaps, that account reconstruction would, if nothing else, keep at bay the randomness that threatened to overwhelm their lives. Then, and in spite of their hesitations about entering into the therapeutic dialogue, those clients whose narratives are included in the following chapters located and restored for themselves a sense of trust and a transformation of identity, albeit at differing levels.

Also central to psychotherapeutic work is the concern with self-autonomy as it is allied with self-definition, an area likewise broached in social research. In *Governing the Soul* Rose explores his interest in narrative control, as it relates to 'the shaping of the private self' (1989, subtitle). He examines the degree to which our intimate lives are truly our own to shape and control, a matter with which each of my clients privately grappled. He argues, more specifically, that psychotherapies have come to shape our subjective experiences by luring us with the promise of 'realigning what we are with what we want to be' (xiii).

> Selves unable to operate the imperative of choice are to be restored through therapy to the status of a choosing individual. Selves who find choice meaningless and their identity constantly fading under inner and outer fragmentation are to be restored, through therapy, to unity and personal purpose. Selves dissatisfied with who they are can engage in therapeutic projects to refurbish and reshape themselves in the directions they desire. The psychotherapies provide technologies of individuality for the production and regulation of the individual who is 'free to choose.' (Rose 1989, 228)

To a significant degree, Rose's comments echoed my clients' early hopes for a successful outcome of their therapeutic process. Most entered therapy with expectations of being 'healed' and of having restored to them a greater sense of direction or mastery.

Such expectations are unrealistic, but they reflect what clients and others have culturally come to anticipate – that healing processes and selves are commodities to be shaped and acted upon. However, this initial fixation with being mended and of viewing the therapist as responsible for the reparation eventually becomes perceived quite differently. Responsibility for change is promptly redirected towards the client in an effort to arrest any further drain on her self-authority. Often such a redirection of accountability by the therapist is interpreted by the client as unwelcome, and even as a frightening level of responsibility. Experiences of sexual exploitation tend to infuse in my clients a state of objectification and consequently obliterate any sense of their having power to alter their own outcome, with the result that self-definition, for those who have been habitually objectified, can seem vast, daunting, and beyond their capacity to achieve. Although we together worked beyond this initial sense of trepidation towards advancing the clients' self-authority, their initial anxiety is a significant impediment to successful therapy that must be surmounted.

Rose's 'technologies of individuality,' of which I am a potential arm, raise concerns for him, as no doubt they do for many engaged in the psychotherapeutic professions. For someone engaged in reconstruction, the degree of personal control that actually exists or is permitted to exist is foremost, but there is a related problem in the character of the techniques themselves, 'through which modern selves are constructed, sustained and remodelled' (1989, xii–xiii).

Rose explains how 'attempts have been made to alter the visible person by acting upon this invisible inner world. Thoughts, feelings and actions may appear as the very fabric and constitution of the intimate self, but they are socially organized and manifested in minute particulars' (1996, 1). His view of the social powers that come to bear upon the person both subscribes to and advances my thinking about my clients' relationships to their account productions and the role that others, including the therapist, perform in the recreation of each story. In this context, Rose's study intersects directly with my own reflexive quest, as a therapist and as a sociologist. I regularly wrestled with my capacity to influence and direct my clients' 'invisible world' and questioned the merit of doing so. Rose has observed what I noted, particularly in the initial stages of my work with clients: 'The government of the soul depends upon our recognition of ourselves as ideally and potentially certain sorts of persons, the unease generated by a normative judgement of what we are and could become, and the incitement offered to overcome this discrepancy by following the advice of experts in the management of the self' (1989, 11). This insight finds a counterpart in the potentially destructive relationship between dominant discourses and my clients' valuation and subsequent shaping of self. It also exposes the practitioner's role as the 'expert' who potentially pressures clients into conformity, to accept 'normative judgements,' and who acts as an uncomfortable reminder for the client to remain aware of any impulse towards steering her in a predetermined direction. However, by sharing with clients our perception of the influence of these dominant discourses, and by aligning social and therapeutic critiques, we can provide a potential antidote to such 'technologies of individuality.' It is by supplementing awareness through persistent work with the client's personal sources of meaning that she ultimately finds enough self-knowledge to enhance her sense of freedom from the dominant discourse that had attempted to portray her.

This theme of socially defined selfhood is also approached by Giddens (1991) from another perspective that is useful for researching therapeutic individual transformations. In his overview of reflexive transformation within the throes of social change, Giddens draws a parallel between the alteration of self and reflexive evolution. He identifies major characteristics of social change that correspond to the intrapersonal transformations we chronicle in therapy. Of these, trust and loss of faith are the issues most in line with my own inquiry. My clients' private experiences merge with the collective phenomenon described by Giddens precisely in the area of dissipated trust and central to his discussion of self reconstruction within a changing social climate. While our work in therapy with trust centres on the intrapersonal, as it radiates outwards to the interpersonal, Giddens is concerned with the global level as it moves inward to affect the individual. In commenting on the collective breakdown of trust in our society, the loss of faith in explanations, and the absence of a predictable source of answers, Giddens observes a general crisis of confidence through which the majority of my clients pass individually:

> In circumstances of uncertainty and multiple choice, the notions of trust and risk have particular application ... Trust established between an infant

and its caretakers provides an 'inoculation' which screens off potential threats and dangers that even the most mundane activities of day-to-day life contain. Trust in this sense is basic to a 'protective cocoon' which stands guard over the self in its dealings with everyday reality. It 'brackets out' potential occurrences which, were the individual seriously to contemplate them, would produce a paralysis of the will, or feelings of engulfment. (1991, 3)

Unwittingly, he describes well the aftermath that the abuse of trust, which characterizes my clients' sexual trauma, has created (1991, 20).

Giddens argues that dissipated trust is a significant dimension of a loss of authority (196). This loss and recasting of external authority, which he identifies as a central aspect of the condition of late modernity, occurs exactly among those who have been sexually exploited. Yet through our therapeutic rebuilding, to echo the words of Giddens, 'the threat of personal meaninglessness is eventually diminished by this reintegration of self and the development of self-trust' (202). This reorganization of the total self commonly takes place among my clients as a necessary part of their reintegration in which the trust that was once projected outwards is consequently relocated inwards. It follows a trauma that has divided my clients within themselves and has separated them from the society that permitted that victimization to occur.

This intrapersonal discovery of symbolic and internally rendered authority has implications for researching the collective pursuit of authority and meaning. Giddens is in accord with this view: 'In the settings of modernity ... the altered self has to be explored and constructed as part of a reflexive process of connecting personal and social change' (1991, 32–3). Coming from the opposite direction, in effect, my clients' personal reworking substantiates his theoretical inroads in this area. Their experiences of intrapersonal fragmentation following abuse stand as testimonials and ground his theory.

Giddens describes the fragmenting effects on the person in the following terms: 'The reflexive project of the self, which consists in the sustaining of coherent yet continuously revised narratives, takes place in the context of multiple choice as filtered through abstract systems' (4). As with Sennett and Rose, his deliberations centre on the social mediation of personal experience and how, under such conditions, self-identity becomes a reflexively organized – though limited – endeavour. This reflexive process creates a fragmented relationship with our embodiment, as the new shaping of the body is increasingly influenced by outside trends. Furthermore, Giddens contends, this process extends 'to the core of the self' (4). In this sense his analysis of reflexive transformation is coupled with the context of my own work, which identifies another way that such intrapersonal accounts are inseparable from the social experience of self.

Giddens's model relies on ideal types to create his thesis and thus necessarily remains remote from the particularities of everyday realities and actual embodiment that the lives of my clients are very much planted in and limited by. While he captures the essence of what is unfolding in the wider world, he potentially overlooks many important distinctions. Giddens does not really define the difference between institutionalized personal ties and the abstract systems of contemporary life. 'Institutionalized personal ties are by their nature abstract ... And while we no doubt do exist in a world of abstract systems, we also exist in a world where the bonds of friendship tie us to special places and people as well as in a world regulated by more institutionalized personal ties' (Seligman 1997, 18). And while Giddens does discriminate between trust in abstract systems and trust in people, he never really reconnects the fissure that his analysis creates. Nevertheless, his general theory concerning the reflexive project of self, while still much removed from the grounded world, illuminates aspects of narrative transformation and affixes a personal process to a collective one.

Sexual Abuse Discourse

My clients' accounts contain pivotal and, at times, culturally uncontaminated insights. They also provide much-needed detail about how the self is transformed at a level to which most of us would not otherwise have access. When viewed collectively, these accounts, and the insights that they embody, illustrate well an important historical phenomenon, or what Plummer describes as 'a shift in consciousness, a recovery through which a negative experience is turned into a positive identity and a private pain becomes part of a political or a therapeutic language' (1995, 50). These ensuing 'political' or 'therapeutic' languages, as I discuss below, hold both advantages and shortcomings for the once sexually abused woman who is attempting to recreate herself.

At the onset of therapy the public definition of my client, who she is, and what has happened to her, has already been externally shaped and defined by her perpetrator, her family, her community, and by more abstract and remote discourses and ideologies. A great many of my clients enter therapy, for example, having read and digested such feminist-inspired popular sexual-abuse literature as *The Courage to Heal* (Bass and Davis 1988), *The Right to Innocence* (Engel 1989), and *The Healing Way* (Kunzman 1990). Significantly, these works address the silencing of women, women and anger, self-esteem and personal power, and other issues of personal politics surrounding sex, gender, and the body. Yet they also raise some remarkably consistent concerns for clients and therapists. The sometimes fixed and hollow descriptions of sexual-abuse survivors represented in this literature mostly objectifies and restrains rather than enables the client in her reconstruction. Though the intention may be to endorse rather than negate her story, this prevailing informed discourse on sexual abuse is also inadvertently an instrument of coercion. Most often its language acts to exercise a form of 'objective' control over her capacity, even to name what had happened to her, thus denying the client a description of her experience in her own terms.

The plethora of literature and media discussion over the past decade and a half reflects the extent to which this subject has become fashionable and even socially inflated. I agree with Plummer that the danger in popularizing sexual abuse rests in producing 'a curious blend of personal talk about experience blended into a distancing language of dysfunctional systems, addiction, "little children within" and trauma – a quasi-objective language reasserting itself over the personal story' (1995, 105). For my part, I have often wondered to what extent my clients were presenting issues in a language and symptomology that had been selected for them by the dominant sexual-abuse rhetoric. Moreover, while these public expressions of concern and the 'distancing' language growing up around them have claimed to uniquely represent the sexual-abuse experience, we found that their remote and generalized depictions, if at all applicable to my clients, were not helpful for understanding the particularities of an individual's plight. My clients and I quickly recognized these 'self-help' approaches as formulaic strategies, and their generalized interpretations and procedures stifle the client's search for the unique solutions necessary for rebuilding her self. Instead the continuous and reflexive nature of my clients' questioning about their own experiences demanded a more rigorous and creative approach than such literature supplied.

To be fair, despite their limitations, this literature and its associated portrayals do provide some clients with an initial, though somewhat abstract, sense of companionship in what is often a lonely and secretive experience. And they do offer a starting point from which to begin the very necessary in-depth work of intrapersonal rebuilding. Such literature assists generally in addressing the victimization of women and girls, allowing clients to place their own violation into the broader social context of a woman's issue. This contextualization normalizes many of their feelings and side-effects, including guilt, fear of telling, and the sublimation of anger often associated with these violations. It also occasionally creates an opening for working with clients' sense of powerlessness, violation, and vulnerability. In these ways, mainstream self-help works have played a helpful social role in popularizing a taboo topic and supporting victims in a general language that speaks to their experience. Consequently, the dilation of this subject has placed a focus on the sexual exploitation of women and attempted to manufacture a strong collective voice for an otherwise socially marginal group.

However, the need to be interpersonally allied and socially accepted is often so great as to propel my clients towards this type of cultural interpretation of their personal experiences before they have formulated and nurtured any substantial private understanding. In this way, they are denied their own authorship. Shearer-Cremean and Winkelmann, in observing this trend in postmodernity, recognize that the 'self is mediated by a variety of community languages' (2004, 5), and such languages, coupled with Rose's 'technologies of individuality,' provide descriptions and even prescriptions for selfhood. Yet when cultural constructions of self are substituted for unique and hence sustainable ones of the client's own creation, whole dimensions of experience are at risk of being ignored or unknown.

The words *survival* and *survivor* are ubiquitous examples of such discursive constructions. They have found a home in the sexual-abuse lexicon and are employed with excessive currency, often quite uncritically, and with little heed to the broader implications of their use. They are the names we interchangeably ascribe to those who have surmounted sexual traumatization. Indeed, it is difficult to read about, discuss, or critically analyse sexual exploitation without encountering the notion of survival. This is partly so because the term, as with the popularization of the subject of sexual abuse in general, has undergone what Orrin Klapp describes as 'social magnification' (1991, 1). As a result of this amplification, none of my clients arrive at the therapeutic doorway completely untouched by the sexual-abuse discourse. It has permeated our culture.

The problematic term *survivor* was added to the sexual-abuse discourse about twenty years ago for the most compelling of reasons. Most importantly, perhaps, it provided feminist theorists and practitioners with a reminder of the parallels between the long-term psychological damages of war and those wrought by gendered violence. Originally, it was a designation, itself indebted to the experience of extermination camp survivors, that vindicated and legitimised the post-war guilt and sufferings of mostly male veterans by giving them attention and credibility (see Bettelheim 1979). Transferring survivor status to the abuse experience was thought to do the same for this most recently designated group of 'victims' (see Herman 1992). There are some clear insights to be garnered, for client and therapist alike, from what has developed in the evolving profile of the survivor. Bruno Bettelheim, Viktor Frankl, and others (Bettelheim 1979; Frankl 1959; Lasch 1984; and others) delineated the process of surviving atrocities in their Holocaust studies, and then feminist literature has tended to draw upon and emphasize studies of Vietnam and other combat veterans, with their accompanying detailed descriptions of the psychological and physiological effects of trauma.

In the view of many, including the majority of my clients, Judith Herman was a pioneer in giving affirmation and extending credence to those who had suffered sexual abuse, through her popularization of the notion that the survival of life-and-death circumstances, such as those in war, and the survival of sexual abuse, shared common after-effects. This equation of abused women with survivors of war aimed to link women to a language that they were otherwise disconnected from, and, at length, to bring a largely female experience into an exchange shared by men and women alike. It validated their individual symptoms by linking them to a wider 'traumatic stress phenomenology.' Consequently, the word *survivor* has succeeded, to a degree, in transporting those who were once abused out of their isolation, secrecy, and silence. The social validation of their trauma has subsequently transformed them into a vocal group. As Herman notes, 'Only after 1980, when the efforts of combat veterans had legitimated the concept of post-traumatic stress disorder, did it become clear that the psychological syndrome seen in survivors of rape, domestic battery, and incest was essentially the same as the syndrome seen in survivors of war' (1992, 32). In fact, much of what constitutes this following collection of post-trauma responses and accounts is common to 'survival' narratives, in whatever form they appear (Des Pres 1980).

There was for many of my clients temporary sustenance in identifying with the common self-description symbolized by *survivor*, despite the frustrations of this label. For better or for worse, it provided them with a link to a 'community language.' It helped them make some sense of their experience and find commonality in what had been a solely private distress. For those reasons, *survivor* remained a useful metaphor through which to consider the client's relationship to her own account.

In her close psycho/textual analysis of the near-death experience of Herman Melville's hero Ishmael, Janet Reno elucidates survivors' tendencies to unite in a common language with the hope of explaining one's experience to oneself and others. This resolve of survivors to break their isolation is one characteristic of her 'paradigm of the survivor.' Reno's model demonstrates what I have noted time and again in my practice and it directly supports, for example, my own observation that the first significant obstacle of survivors is 'a painful sense of isolation.' Reno sees this isolation as coupled with 'an overwhelming sense of chaos' and 'a feeling that no longer is there order in the world.' She further isolates guilt, followed by loss, and finally mourning, as the second and third thresholds they must cross. Most importantly, according to Reno, we must consider the loss of the innocent untraumatized self that 'died' as a result of the tragedy (1990, 31). Reno views these problems, especially the last, as ones through which each survivor passes and, in so doing, finds a way to reconstruct the self by becoming the ultimate creator of her own narrative. The narrative in this way becomes a powerful tool of rehabilitation.

Reno suggests too that 'during the disaster itself, a willingness to merge with something greater than oneself can be crucial' (1990, 38). This observation attests to and partially explains the social bridging that all of my clients sought. Following trauma, such inclusion in survivorship allowed them to draw from a collective strength in order to mend a long-felt isolation. It also explains their initial adoption of ill-fitting externally manufactured descriptions of their exploitations. Despite the risk of raising internal contradictions for the client, the inclination to share personal experiences of abuse with others is pervasive.

Reno's analysis of the distinctions between *survivor* and what she calls 'survivorship' illuminates an enveloping tendency towards inclusion. Yet it proposes a perspective on survival that is different from the therapeutic literature on sexual abuse. She offers insights into why so many who were sexually abused might initially and willingly adopt the self-description 'survivor' in an optimistic act of self-transformation and then subsequently feel frustrated by the lack of significant constructive change in their sense of self. This happened because identifying oneself as a survivor, or locating oneself within a popular discourse, does little by itself to ensure that one's injuries will be adequately attended to. Yet those previously violated are at first unaware of this shortcoming.

In my practice, I have been a regular witness to such internal discontent. With a new-found identification as survivor, former victims initially no longer consider themselves victims. They expect that much of their work toward recovery has already been accomplished merely through this name shift. Stripped of its associations, however, *survivor* is little more than a hollow analytical label, no better or worse than other objectifications. Before she has entered therapy, the reality that little has changed by leaving one classification and adopting another generally leaves the client feeling thwarted, frustrated, and without insight into her reaction.

Why does this happen? Reno provides a rationale:

> The rebirth of the individual required by full survivorship is by no means inevitable. To pass through a disaster and to survive is one kind of event; to pass from psychic numbing into feeling again is another, more extended experience. The first is emotional and historical, the second is metaphysical. Greater courage may be required for survivorship, or adjustment to survival, than for survival itself. For the most part, one has relatively little choice during a disaster as to one's survival. Presumably those who did not survive disasters also intended to remain alive. Surviving is a matter of instinct. But survivorship requires one to accept one's survivor guilt, to live through boundless grief, to endure the disorder of memory in a search for new order, and to mourn the dead and one's own dead self. Survivorship, though it may involve the instincts, also includes another element: extraordinary courage. Survivorship stories highlight what is best in humankind. (1990, 45–6)

Reno does not equate survival with the act of healing, as so many do. In her interpretation, the word *survivor* actually loses the power and status that it was intended to possess, because survival is taken for granted.

The work that is necessary following survival is intense, intraper-sonal, and without guarantee of a successful outcome. In Reno's view, survival is little more than a circumstance, and a past one at that. Instead, her idea of 'survivorship' is, in contrast, rooted in self-reclama-tion and the hard work of personal reparation. When integrated and constructively repossessed, survivorship represents a present and reflexive process of change. Importantly, the onus for transformation in Reno's analysis, as in our therapeutic work, is the individual's.

Problems of External Constructions of Survival

What, if anything, is forfeited by the sexually exploited person who opts for mainstream descriptions of her intensely personal experience? As noted, the greater social connection offered to those who have simi-larly suffered serves, albeit temporarily, to mollify a sense of alienation. Yet Plummer (1995) cautions that one result can also be the victim's desensitization that results from a bombardment of stories. This social connection can diminish the original aim for many victims: a heighten-ing of sensitivity in confronting the past. The downside of such popu-larization of sexual-abuse issues has also been well summarized by Klapp, who is concerned with the extreme reactions that often follow such a public outpouring of stories:

> Contagious communications spread rapidly and thoughtlessly, and lead to extremes and exaggerations that are later often seen to be follies. In this sense they make much out of little, magnify little into seeming much. After which they fade or burst like bubbles. This is what we denote when we speak of rumors, stampedes, panics, hysterias, mobs, riots, fads, crazes, manias, booms, bubbles. Their time is brief but their curve of growth is exponential, as with disease epidemics. (1991, 61)

In this public climate, distortions can ultimately discredit the legiti-macy of the victim's experience. Most notably, such representation has presented itself as an organized discrediting of sexual-abuse accounts under the auspices of 'false memory syndrome,' which has surfaced alongside publicized attempts to give these stories credibility. In its feverish pursuit of accessible explanations and categorizations, the public appears to be entirely capable of making trite what is vital to the private person. Therefore, the popularization of the abuse experience can displace victimized women from their own stories by seconding and making mainstream their carefully rendered private touchstones. This is why possession needs to be restored to them in a form and a language of their own making.

While mainstream messages were alluring to a number of my clients, most eventually agreed that such remote and externally rendered designs had little sustaining power. Each client's emerging account illustrated the tension between subjective and discursively rendered descriptions of self and ultimately countered these external efforts to characterize the abuse experience by giving expression to the client's own voice and momentarily freeing her from peripheral controls. As I mentioned earlier, my client's initial sense of identity is rooted in a broader discourse. Her self-characterization is, in this sense, controlled from without. This is why her re-appropriation of authorship is important. Indeed, the central issue raised by her therapeutic narrations is that individual authorship is imperative, because the voice of the author needs to be restored as an index of authenticity. The client must not leave her abuse to mere discourse to define from without. Her objective is to understand from within what has happened to her. To do so she must resort to her own symbols against the backdrop and pressure of this public discourse.

Therapeutically imposing a definition such as 'survivor,' for example, denies someone who has been exploited the autonomy and control that is fundamental to her reconstruction. One after-effect of sexual abuse is vacillation, in the wake of abuse, between an extreme mistrust and fear of others and an unrealistic belief in the implicit trustworthiness of those closest to them, so the client's trust in the therapist can at times be unevaluated and extreme. Because of this characteristic dilemma, it is unrealistic to assume that those who adopt the self-description 'survivor' offered by their therapist are making this decision from a grounded perspective of self-assurance, personal insight, and free choice.

The form of 'survivor' that is applied to sexual exploitation promises acceptance by and admission to a dialogue created mostly by women. The siren beckons most alluringly for those who have been sexually abused to embrace this designation and hence this social assemblage as their own. *Reach for the Rainbow*, a popular sexual-abuse recovery guide, for example, begins as follows: 'Congratulations! If you have been sexually or physically abused and you are reading this book, you are a survivor' (Finney 1992, 15). However, the label survivor, in the sexual abuse context, carries with it a whole host of connotations, as well as an obligation to pursue a specified path of recovery. Yet these requirements are not immediately recognizable as such. Nor is it readily apparent that the options available to survivors are extremely limited. The unstated implication of this categorization is that the sexually abused person must leap certain social hurdles in order to merit this name. To be a 'survivor,' for instance, carries with it the intimation that one must pursue therapy and/or follow self-help literature.

Is a person who was abused destined to remain a victim until she has engaged with the therapeutic? Is she still worthy of the title 'survivor' if she designs her own method of attending to her psychic fractures, privately and in her own terms? Is she a 'survivor' if she does not adopt the popular language that describes and contains her experience? Apparently not. Bass and Davis argue, 'No matter how committed you are, it is extremely difficult to heal from child sexual abuse in isolation ... It is essential that you have at least one other person with whom you can share your pain and your healing. The person may be another survivor, a member of a support group, or a counsellor' (1988, 22).

While there must be some individuals for whom reintegration can occur without therapeutic intervention or self-help literature, these are obviously not the people I saw in my practice. Rather, in their initial thinking, my clients reflected what Bass and Davis recommended. Many arrived in therapy content to place their reconstruction in my hands. They consistently stated their expectations of the therapeutic process in the language of the sexual-abuse discourse that now permeates our culture. For those who have been sexually exploited, the awareness of such a seemingly well-established network of 'experts' and 'texts' cautions them against directing themselves, unassisted, through the recovery maze. They presume that such an organized alliance must know, as they never alone could, what avenues they should follow and how their recovery should take shape. Nonetheless, therapists' and clients' uncritical application of mainstream discourse to individual reparations poses fundamental threats that question the expectations and efficacy of therapy.

The war of semantics (Bolker 1995) that rages around victims in the popular sexual-abuse literature may only drain their power and lead them further away from their needs and final goals. Consequently, one might argue, for women, much has been sacrificed in these public negotiations. Some of my clients, when seeking therapy, had already endured such a prolonged and devastating loss of control that they do not know where to begin taking back some direction for themselves, and they commonly grant the therapist authority in place of self-governance. Such external influence introduces the potential for stunting the development of clients' creative problem-solving techniques and, more generally, their autonomy. Therapeutic interference can be problematic for still other reasons. The most critical of these hazards for the client is, as Giddens puts it, in 'taking refuge in a dominant authority' because this is 'essentially an act of submission (1991, 196). Since one of the most corrosive effects of sexual violation is rooted in its victim's forced submission, she actually risks recreating in therapy the effects of that original abuse. In this sense a decisive aspect of the account's restorative power lies in its capacity to reinstate some authority to its teller. However, if the client in her reconstructive process is once again compelled to relinquish control to some outside entity, she will at best be stalled in her endeavour to heal.

Over time and with the strengthening of my clients' own insights, the authority of public discourse over their experiences often came to be viewed as unenlightening, and even personally alienating. Smith notes though, 'We [as women] have assented to this authority and can withdraw our assent' – a response that is 'essential to the making of knowledge, culture, and ideology based on the experiences and relevances of women (1987, 18). Rejecting an uncritical espousal of characterizations emanating from self-help literature, or for that matter any categorization that has not been vetted by the client, represents the client's refusal to allow her reality to be constructed once again by another. Such trust in her own constructions and interpretations constitutes a tremendous leap into the unfamiliar, especially for one who has only ever known a reality that has been consistently defined by others. Initially, at least, prevailing public characterizations of sexual victimization are alluring because they afford an obtainable structure and are grounded in a sense of community. At some point in their progression toward integration, however, my clients favour a more internally rendered self-representation of their experience above all others, as the apparatus for combating their state of solitude, marginalization, degradation, and fear.

The definition of survival, as it applies to an individual's ability to surmount wartime atrocities, has become a fixed script when it is used to define the experience of sexual assault. A major drawback to this strategy is, as Plummer notes, that 'much of modern life is ... trapped in the conventions and rituals of pre-existing stories which prevent, conceal, and block other ways of seeing' (1995, 127). Therapists Anderson and Goolishian also refuse to accept the assumed value in such classifications. 'Our view holds that each problem description, each understanding, each treatment is unique to the communicating realities in which we participate. These realities are always in flux and never stay the same' (1988, 386). If our clients' realities are perpetually changing, as indeed they are, why must the guidelines for their recovery, as laid out in much of the sexual-abuse literature, remain static? From the standpoint of the therapist, fixed descriptions of sexual abuse and survivorship are problematic and they eventually limit the horizon for therapist and client alike.

Several serious problems thus lie in wait for the therapist who opts for a blanket adoption of pre-existing definitions for describing what she is seeing. Here, Anderson and Goolishian are helpful in defining the root problem:

> Pre-assigned labels that we often use to understand our work get in the way of collaborative problem defining, and they often describe and create problems that we cannot work with ... It is never helpful to create, or freeze in apodictic certainty, a problem definition that defies new meaning or conversational change. In monological conversation, that is, when an idea or aggregate of ideas dominates, new co-created understanding, new shared narrative, and mutual change become increasingly impossible. (1988, 38)

My practice and research has borne out the strength of this observation. Rigidly adhered to categorizations stunt creativity. The danger in favouring them over an evolving critical and reflexive process is that existing definitions render inactive the potential breadth of our perceptions and close down other ways of seeing.

In this regard, Denzin sees an additional problem tied to the blanket adoption of one-size-fits-all prescriptions. He notes the frequent disparity between the general label and the individual experience:

> These constructions may draw upon media or popular cultural representations and may or may not reflect actual experiences. When they do not reflect lived experience, the gap between the real and its representations becomes existentially problematic. In such moments ideology repressively intrudes into the worlds of lived experience. (1992, 90)

It is often the case that such constructions, though developed for the most stellar of reasons, become intrinsically fickle. Anderson and Goolishian offer an observation in this regard. 'It has interested us for some time that psychological problems seemingly appear, change shape, and disappear as therapists' vocabularies and descriptions change' (1988, 385). In short, the priority must be to see through the discourse to the essence of the client's meaning. While there is a danger of prematurely dispensing with popular sexual-abuse literature, as it might still be serving a purpose for the client, these fixed descriptions are ultimately not in the client's best interests. For they leave her in a passive state, they shut down her capacity for creative self-interpretation, they deny her the power to design her own solutions, and they offer a hyper-reality, to borrow from Baudrillard, in place of a self-mediated reality.

A New Basis for Understanding

During the course of self-reparation, clients become more open to considering alternative perspectives, and they re-evaluate the traditional basis of internal and external validity. As part of this process sources formally invested with authority are increasingly deemed inadequate as arbitrators of clients' personal experiences. Accompanying this displacement there emerges a general unwillingness to invest an unqualified trust in anyone, by mere virtue of the social roles he fills. In effect, my clients' growing discernment elicited my recognition of and respect for them as a fundamental source of validity, and was a catalyst in their reparation. Our micro exploration of how and from where this new source of trust springs grounds Giddens's and Sennett's assertion that all forms of trust, whether they are rendered locally or socially, are resurrected on shifting sands. Trust is no longer perceived as a permanent and certain entity but, instead, as a continuous development in the construction of self.

The validity of my former clients' experiences of sexual exploitation is fixed to this matter of trust and transfer in authority. The impact of the public demand on a private story to provide *the* truth, in the case of our work, produced, first, a struggle to conform to an externally wrought definition of validity before the client located worth and satisfaction in a privately rendered description. Through the hard work of self-definition, the client's experience eventually superseded in value the publicly manufactured discourse. The most important standard of validity by which to access these narratives thus became what each client found significant and personally bearable. This result upholds Smith's reminder that a woman's lived experience must stand as a relative truth:

> The method of experience returns us always to the subject active in remembering, in finding out how to speak from the actualities of her life, bringing forward what was into a speaking for which she is the only authority. It is a method that feminists have taken up in a variety of ways. For me it established a place to situate a subject as knower of a sociology that might explore how her life is put together by relations and forces that are not fully available to her experiencing. (1990c, 5)

These 'forces' that 'put together' my former clients' lives called for a tangible proof of truth about their sexual-abuse claims. The strength of this demand perpetuated in the client a split between self- and social perceptions of that self. In Smith's view, the problematic was that women most typically live outside of the powerful dialogue that shapes our society: 'Women have been largely excluded from the work of producing the forms of thought and the images and symbols in which thought is expressed and ordered' (1987, 18). The 'truth' that was expected of their accounts therefore was not necessarily their own. In fact, it was uniformly concluded among my clientele that in some respects we were all – client, therapist, and reader alike – to some degree caught up in appealing to a universal standard by which to assess, legitimize, and categorize personally and socially upsetting material. It therefore remained vital that in therapy, at the very least, the accounts of exploited women were not weighed and measured against an external definition of 'truth' that they have had no hand in creating.

This feminist message is borne out in the body of social research that looks at a woman's standpoint, and/or her 'voice' (Gilligan 1982, 2002), and how this voice has been culturally suppressed. As already discussed in my introduction, it is crucial to our understanding of the therapeutic context, because the sexual abuse of women and children has thrived and continues to thrive under a dynamic of patriarchy, privacy, and silence. As long as this is so, establishing the validity of these women's experiences will remain an elusive task, even to them.

A feminist perspective furthermore provides a framework for addressing the client's personal concerns about inequality and powerlessness, and conversely, equality and empowerment. Understanding sexuality, as a far-reaching social phenomenon, steeped in power and gender, assists the victim in depersonalizing her abuse and, in turn, alleviating some of her associated guilt. But she needs to integrate a genuine understanding of these issues in order for her to establish a firmer structure upon which to rebuild a fractured identity.

Apart from questions of truth and validity in sexual-abuse accounts, my specific focus is additionally on how abuse is experienced, synthesized, reconstructed, and expressed by individual women. I share Gilligan's interest in the intricacies of such processes, 'in the interaction of experience and thought, in different voices and the dialogues to which they give rise, in the way we listen to ourselves and others, in the stories we tell about our lives' (1982, 2). Her explorations have overlapped with my own, in our concern with the presence of 'different voices' and their role in the project of re-authoring the self. Gilligan focuses especially on the differences between women's experiences and formal thinking about human development, and how these differences are rooted in gender constructions. While I accept this view, I also diverge from Gilligan by wanting to plunge beneath the social surface to consider the value of the metaphorical and symbolic expressions of a client's voice, her silences, and the new personally rendered sense of self that she forms through a changing self-definition and self-description.

My main concern, as a sociologist/therapist, however, is to examine the intertwining of the personal and social aspects of my clients' self-expression, and the nature of their continuing quest, which we sought by locating its motivation and form through narration and reflexive dialogue. The communication of subjective meanings is difficult for my clients, though necessary, and represents an ongoing challenge for me as a researcher, for because of the difficulties in transcribing complex experiences, we risk objectifying and formalizing these communications by removing them 'from the course of everyday happenings, providing it with significant form after the fact' (Smith 1987, 48). Doing so obviously distorts the sense of personal validity that my clients established for themselves. Thus, I have attempted to avoid the kind of objectification to which Smith refers by encouraging my clients to express, recognize, and accept that personal sense of authenticity derived from their own experiences. Ultimately, each client must tell her own story her way.

Because sociological enquiry has directed me to questions about whether or not narrative control is real or illusionary, and whether the account's outcome is an internal rendering or, to a large extent, an expertly manipulated process, it has also influenced my perspective on the validity of my clients' narratives and my decision to position myself as researcher and observer squarely within the experience of my clients – a placement that fits naturally with my role as therapist. Finally, feminist sociology, in particular, has confirmed my own insiders' perspective as legitimate, despite a traditional sociological tendency to view the legitimacy of experience from the outside looking in.

In the chapters that follow, I discuss the therapeutic and sociological ideas that have most influenced my work with my clients – they are presented in and around my clients' own accounts. In viewing therapeutic narratives through a sociological lens, we gain a more diverse and in-depth look at the issues that emerge from the evolution of the private experience of sexual violation and towards their public expression. My commentary therefore weaves in and out of their accounts, denoting my reflexive quest, as therapist and researcher.

2 Locating the Self: The Language of Survival

Jesse sought therapy in order to address the effects of childhood incest by her alcoholic father and sexual assaults by other male relatives and neighbours. At the time of entering therapy she was approaching her fortieth birthday. Jesse then suffered from depression and sleeplessness, complicated by debilitating migraines. She had been attempting to suppress these afflictions with anti-depressant medication and painkillers for much of her adult life. Nevertheless she carried with her what she described as an almost bottomless sense of grief that she identified as stemming from 'a many-edged loss.' Such a pronounced feeling of loss as Jesse's is a frequent characteristic of those who have suffered and surmounted sexual trauma (see Herman 1992).

Jesse grew up as the eldest girl in an extremely impoverished rural Newfoundland family with nine children. Poverty and the chaos brought about by alcoholism and physical violence in her home rendered Jesse vulnerable to incest, which, as a result of this environment, also remained unacknowledged in her surroundings (Stanko 1990, 85). In her daily world there was little chance of refuge from the emotional unpredictability that defined her existence. Even her physical surroundings were overtly and subtly unsafe. She described, for instance, sleeping, as a child, on a seat that had been removed from an abandoned car. A parachute left behind by the American forces at a nearby army base served as her blanket. Jesse recalled her fear when lying awake listening to rats moving in the springs of her car-seat bed. As an adult, she carried a lingering sense of urgency, among other things, about needing to keep her hands and feet tucked under her blankets and away from the edge of the bed.

Jesse described growing up in an environment that, from her very earliest recollections, was physically and emotionally dangerous and riddled with personal losses. For her, the problem of isolation was ever present, since the abuse she endured seemed both indescribable and personally threatening to translate. Often, others expressly did not want to know of it. Jesse, for example, maintained that her mother was unwilling to hear of her husband's acts of incest toward Jesse and exhibited no real concern for her daughter's pain. While Jesse felt that her mother ultimately 'used' her claims of incest 'as a way out' of her own 'violent marriage,' she paid them no heed beyond that aim. This outcome left Jesse alienated from the only apparently 'safe' adult relationship in her family.

Her incest experience began at the age of eight and ended at age eleven when her mother took her to the police. As if to confirm Jesse's social and emotional marginalization, when the police investigated the abuse allegations they told Jesse directly that they did not believe her story. The case was closed, her mother never made mention of it again, and in her shame and sense of betrayal, nor did Jesse. That is the point at which, for Jesse, the incest stopped. She did not know at the time that her father had begun sexually molesting her younger sister, the one closest to Jesse in age. This denial and dismissal of Jesse's experience by her mother, and then the police, perpetrated for Jesse a long-term and painful emotional isolation that was rooted in her father's sexual abuse of her.

In this chapter I consider Jesse's account as a reflexive process composed by her, guided by me, and aimed at overcoming the conditions that had essentially paralysed her intra- and inner rebuilding. Jesse's account illustrates many of my clients' relationships to the label 'survivor,' as outlined in the last chapter, or more generally to the dominant discourse that has grown up around their suffering and purports to describe and offer solutions for it.

At the onset of therapy, some self-help, sexual-abuse literature and its accompanying language found a ready audience in Jesse, as it spoke to her about the need to nurture and heal herself, and assured her that others had suffered similar abuses. Jesse was proud to be associated with the term *survivor*. In essence, it touched her through her isolation, it offered her a greater connection, and it left her temporarily buoyant. But the generalizations and prescriptions that this general body of literature offered could not sustain her. The models for healing left little room for her development of unique solutions. Before Jesse could freely benefit from her reflexive process of reconstruction, she first needed to separate herself from others' constructions of her experience. She needed also to locate for herself the issues that most impeded her progress. Ironically, for Jesse, and for many of my clients, an inability to feel and react like other 'survivors' she read about or saw interviewed on television registered as yet another instance of her personal failure in a long line of many.

The ensuing sections focus on our therapeutic work, leading up to the deeply reflexive analysis that typically characterizes the last portion of my therapeutic exchanges with clients. Parts of Jesse's narrative are woven throughout this discussion in order both to concretize the process of therapy for my reader and to anchor this clearly social issue of sexual abuse in a local and personal form. I trace her evolution, through therapy, by relating and comparing her story to the term *survivor*. I use this word as a metaphor for the many words, descriptions, and images that combine to manufacture the textually mediated experience that attempts to define my clients' experiences of personal violation and exploitation. In the ensuing discussion I also consider, what the adoption of this label had to offer her and what more it seemed to promise, yet did not fulfil. Finally, I examine how aligning herself with this social construction may have stalled Jesse's reparation by alluring her with a ready-made formula, a 'recipe knowledge' (Berger and Luckmann 1966, 65) for recovery.

Jessie's Search for Meaning and Coherence

Like Melville's Ishmael, Jesse outlived the experiences of cruelty, exploitation, and death that had surrounded her and directly touched her. Her physical self endured, despite overt neglect and abuse, and her own dangerous sense of disconnection from her body. She struggled to regenerate her depressed existence, first through prescription medicine and eventually in various forms of therapy. Her following account is a manifest representation of her choice to live beyond merely surviving. Through this medium Jesse attempted to conquer personal isolation, fear, external and internal chaos, and a multitude of losses.

In therapy, despite her belief that she had little jurisdiction over her life, Jesse began to construct her therapeutic account quite deliberately. Jesse told her story with skill and urgency. Initially, she relayed several of her darkest memories haltingly and in still-life form. Then she brought forward, at her own pace and of her own choosing, more verbal snapshots. Graphic and emotionally charged depictions of certain episodes of her life followed. While she spoke of a 'greyness' that continuously threatened to consume her, her own voice eventually overpowered these negative preoccupations and they were reconstructed in a new and more bearable form. A sense of necessity was evident as her slow unveiling eventually became a rapid-fire style of transmission. This change stemmed partially from the sense of release that she had found in narration. And in my audience she found the companionship that she had craved, but that her abuse had previously disallowed.

In 'The Unnamable' Samuel Beckett writes of the unstoppable power of voice and its force in sustaining a will to remain in the present, despite the inner torments that haunt us from the past. His cast of seemingly disembodied voices grasp desperately from their respective states of isolation for a greater sense of connection. The plight of Beckett's characters is one that my clients, and Jesse in particular, know well. These characters, like many of my clients, feel an urgency to give expression to their experiences, and in doing so to avoid being consumed by their past. The secretive nature of my clients' abuses had kept them locked in their past and estranged from their social worlds. The witnessed therapeutic account, however, provided a renewed connection. This association kept them in the present, from where they could focus their energies on their own search for meaning and the recovery of things lost to them.

Below, the disembodied voice of Beckett's unnamed narrator and the words that he creatively organizes represents one solution for breaking through the isolation.

> I can't go on, you must go on, you must say the words as long as there are any, until they find me, until they say me, strange pain, strange sin, you must go on, perhaps it's done already, perhaps they have said me already, perhaps they have carried me to the threshold of my story, before the door that opens on my story, that would surprise me, if it opens, it will be I, it will be the silence, where I am, I don't know, I'll never know, in the silence you don't know, you must go on, I can't go on, I'll go on. (Beckett 1965, 414)

My clients, like Beckett's characters, struggle to describe themselves apart from a social characterization. They speak in order to break the isolation shaped by a silence that had dominated them. The overwhelming inclination to do so brought them into therapy despite fears of not being believed, of feeling ashamed, of assuming responsibility for what had happened to them, and, even potentially, of not being safe with the person(s) to whom they chose to relate their past experience. The immediate necessity of reframing the sexual exploitation in their words was intense and social. It was by initiating an expression of her multiple exploitations that Jessie broke her social and intrapersonal isolation. In doing so, she remembered her former 'untraumatized self,' and began to recognize some worthwhile aspects of herself and her history. Accordingly, this shift restored to her some resilience and energy with which to battle ongoing depression and low self-esteem.

The point at which therapy is chosen generally marks the client's first conscious move, after a traumatic experience, toward both autonomy and an enhanced sense of personal control. But to experience a sense of having surpassed her ordeal does not happen as simply or as quickly as some literature suggests. Nor is this stage reached if her self-description is manipulated by the therapist. Rather, ever-evolving reflexive exchanges and soliloquies form the foundations from which new insights and eventually personal control spring.

At the outset of therapy, Jesse presented her story in the random, snapshot fashion typical of survivors of disasters in a stage of traumatic memory, which Herman describes as 'wordless and static' (1992, 175). Indeed, Jesse relayed to me memories that seemed motionless. They stood alone, devoid of emotional content, and they were literally recalled to her in the form of old black-and-white photographs. Jesse was disturbed by this fact, and she repeatedly stressed that all of her memories were recollected only 'in black and white.'

Significantly, this therapeutic relationship also marked the first time for her that Jesse permitted herself to be vulnerable and was not consequently abused. Her unprecedented openness with me, and my respect for her, together eventually granted in Jesse the needed sense of safety for her to visit both negative and positive memories in more detail. As her confidence in the therapeutic relationship grew, so did the quality and degree of her self-disclosure. She accordingly began presenting dreams for discussion that contained some colour, but they too were primarily remembered in black, white, and shades of grey.

As Jesse's experience suggests, descriptions of abuse often begin as little more than disconnected images that resemble postcards and are empty of all emotional expression. The teller seems resigned to the knowledge that neither she nor her trauma can be adequately captured here. As the integration proceeds, however, her memories may become once again infused with sensory details. This is a time characterized by emotional chaos (see Herman 1992). It is also a phase of continuous mental and emotional activity. Contrary to what the term *survivor* contends, in no way is it static or an experience of the past. Only personal fortitude and creativity allow this process to unfold, for feelings of concentrated and continuing chaos are often evident. That is the downside of this stage, as dreadful memories from the past randomly invade the present. Just as the personal fragmentation experienced in times of disaster or abuse does not occur coherently, neither are memories of disintegration recalled in that way (Wiesel 1990).

When the incest first began, sleeping between her brothers sometimes brought Jesse short-term safety from her father's nightly visits to her bed. When she was a little older, she tried keeping him away by leaning her bed against her bedroom door. This was not usually very effective for, as Jesse said, 'I couldn't lock the door because I didn't have a door handle.' The hole in the door where the handle should have been was an image that revisited her in her nightmares, as an adult. It was through this hole that she would watch for her father's dreaded appearance.

A feeling of being out of control was a consuming sensation for Jesse at the onset of therapy. She repeatedly questioned the frequency of sexual violations in her childhood that she recalled, she wondered if there was more she couldn't recall, and she disparaged herself for her incapacity to stop them. Her overriding sense of guilt came from a belief that she was herself somehow responsible for having invited these assaults. Because of her numerous perpetrators, both from inside and outside of her family, Jesse also worried that, for the abuse to have happened this often to her, she must have sought it in some way. Elana Newman, in her work on narrative and childhood sexual abuse, supplies a rationale for re-victimization that is rooted in the original objectification of the child. She writes, 'Sexual abuse communicates that the victim is an object used for someone else's sexual needs. Such meta-communications may become integrated into the child's evolving self-concept so that the survivor's identity is obscured and subsumed as an entity whose purpose is to serve others (2004, 24).

Questions such as why has this happened to me? and why by so many different people? plague most who have been victimized (Haugaard and Reppucci 1989, 240). They are queries that must find some resolution in order to free the client to move on to other issues that may be impeding her reconstruction. While we visited these problems repeatedly, the understandings could not be externally imposed as they needed to be first uncovered and magnified from within. Jesse was in this sense no exception. She felt that she was somehow destined for continued sexual victimization. This left her feeling afraid, vulnerable, and out of control, in public and in private spaces. Given these conditions, clarity surrounding the issue of her abuse was difficult for Jesse to achieve, let alone maintain. She eventually found a piece of the answer by looking back at her chaotic home environment that first permitted this abuse to occur. She realized that, if she could not have found protection from incest within her own home, it made sense that there would be faint prospects for protection from the dangers of the wider community. For as indicated, Jesse's exploitations had been numerous and had extended beyond familial abuse.

Jesse said that she had once been a straight-A student, that is 'until grade six, when everything fell apart.' This marked the point at which she found herself unable to bridge the discrepancy between the abuses of home and her persona of success at school. Her facade crumbled, and she fell, academically and socially, to the bottom of her class. Her growing social isolation undermined her still further by contributing to an indescribable inner void. In constructing and reconstructing her account, Jesse relocated these distinct before- and after-abuse selves. In this discovery, she recognized that then, unlike now, she had felt herself proficient and more confident within her public world.

The skill of Jesse's therapeutic account construction came from many years of mentally replaying the story in an attempt to make some sense out of the chaos of her life. From her state of relative social isolation she had practised the telling and re-sorting of details from her past many times before seeking therapy. Yet, as indicated above, what initially emerged in therapy was not close to a thorough accounting. Instead this intrapersonal work amounted initially to only a skeletal reconstruction. Nevertheless this was the way in which Jesse made her experience first bearable and later presentable. It was also a method that she had come to on her own. In this way her social isolation had served a purpose by forcing her to call upon her own ingenuity for sources of endurance. It also provided her with the insight that her growing yet still fragile sense of freedom from exploitation was something that she had begun to develop at a much earlier age, through reading and fantasy. Intellectual pursuits had always played an important role in her ability to endure incest and a violent family life. And later, reading and authorship injected hope into what she felt had been a death-in-life existence.

To Jesse, the significance of recollection in mostly colourless, snap-shot-like dreams and memories meant that she could feel somewhat removed from her memories; it was as if she were 'watching a movie' or 'looking at someone else's pictures.' She did not feel that she was responsible for their content. This sense of remove permitted Jesse some control as she escorted me through events and places that she had never before entered with another person.

The first dream fragment that Jesse recalled in therapy illustrates this. Through it she introduced the window in her home that figured prominently in her earliest memories of incest. 'I wake up in a grey light. There is an evil presence all around me. I look out the window. It is the same window I looked out of while my father was abusing me. I see a blue car driving up the hill. Elvis Presley is driving the car.' In this dream, Jesse was referring symbolically to her sense of not being in the driver's seat – she did not feel in control of the course that her life was taking. Indeed, Elvis Presley, a remote superstar, was the one in control. She told me that he represented hope to her.

This escape image of the blue car, as she characterized it, and the dream's lone source of colour, represented the only release from the dream's overriding sense of evil. Although she had not acknowledged it before she had this dream, fantasy and imagination had provided Jesse's sole source of escape from her harsh reality. As with her earlier fantasies, Jesse projected onto this Elvis figure the attributes that she herself needed to incorporate in order to take over the project of her own repair (Jung 1974, 50). Jesse said she viewed Elvis as 'sad and lonely like [her] self.' Yet 'he was strong too.' However, he possessed a strength that Jesse did not yet have access to in herself. Through our further analysis, this dream provided Jesse with the awareness that she would not be able to project onto another the task of her own reconstruction and that her strength and her solutions could not be externally constructed if they were to be personally effective. Taking this message with us, we began our in-depth work in earnest.

Jesse's strongest memories of her father's incest were of him standing behind her, fondling her, and performing sexual intercourse on her, while she faced a window from inside their home. Through the window, while this was happening to her, Jesse watched children playing outside. She explained, 'I didn't know what he was doing to me, I never looked.' She did know that she 'longed to be free like the other children.' She could hear 'their games and laughter' and tuned into them as a way of 'escaping from [her] present nightmare.' During those deeply unhappy years, Jesse had 'tried everything [she] could think of' to keep away from her father's assaults. She never fully came to the realization that they were beyond her control, perhaps because such a realization would have made them unbearable. But, in revisiting her violations, she began to view her childish attempts at evasion as a precious dimension of her reclamation and reparation. They signified to her an unwillingness to be a part of this abuse, and much later, memories of these tactics helped her to absolve herself of guilt.

At age fifteen, Jesse became a mother to the first of her two children. At this same time her mother died and Jesse took over the parenting of her half-sister, her mother's youngest child. This tremendous responsibility complicated enormously her longing for freedom. The premature loss of her mother left her with the responsibility of raising these children while she was still in need of mothering herself. Her mother's death also closed any potential for resolution between her and her mother. Her mother's refusal to acknowledge Jesse's abuse was a painful fissure that could not be directly confronted. Jesse's mounting desperation thus grew out of a sense of hopelessness coupled with a belief that her only promise of parental love and security was now gone.

Later in therapy, as a way of coping with the loss of her mother and her own despair, Jesse resurrected and nurtured one rare and fragile connection to a sense of stability that she could remember from her childhood. This memory represented a tranquil time in her day-to-day life as a child when her mother was at home and Jesse was temporarily free from her father's sexual assaults. She remembered,

> I would leave the bedroom door open a crack to see the light from the rest of the house and to hear my mother doing the supper dishes. As a child, this was my only safe time because my mother was at home being a mother and I was safe from my father's assaults as long as my bedroom door was open.

This memory had great significance for several reasons. Foremost, it was the only recollection Jesse had of routine and predictability in her family environment. This scene represented a rare and temporary relief from chaos. In contrast to this fragment Jesse recalled most other episodes of family contact as erratic and threatening – memories that left her with little more than feelings of panic and a lack of continuity. In comparison, this more tranquil memory was far more emotionally and intellectually complex. It was, for example, initially noteworthy to Jesse

for its lack of colour. In this and other ways it resembled the emotionally buffered and somewhat removed atmosphere of her dreams. This
memory took place at dusk, or as Jesse recalled it, 'the time between the
lights.' This time of day was when Jesse returned to 'an internal source,'
from which she drew sustenance for endurance.

Twilight continued to bring Jesse solace as an adult. Once long
removed from the dangers of her father's abuse, she came to experience
her association with this dusk-time ritual as deeply complex. Foremost
it was a time for inner reflection. Jesse described how as an adult she
would still sometimes lie in her bed at this time of day and listen 'to the
sounds of children between the lights. The sounds of their voices are so
clear at this time. The sound hurts me with a physical pain. It reminds
me of my abuse but also I could not live without that sound ... it is so
important to me to hear children play.' These sounds represented the
freedom from burden and pain that Jesse had longed for as a child, yet
remained forever elusive to her. Nevertheless, her desire to have that
wish realized sustained her during her childhood abuse and later, as an
adult. It filled her with a mixed sense of longing and hope.

Jesse had lived most of her life feeling immobilized and unable to
stave off unwanted sexual advances from men; they held power over
her, by virtue of their physical size or their position of authority (Stanko
1990, 86). She frequently inquired, during our therapeutic discourses,
whether she had 'victim stamped on [her] forehead,' and if this was
why she was repeatedly assaulted. She regularly expressed another
reoccurring sense of having 'no control over [her] body' (Featherstone,
Hepworth, and Turner 1991, 95). She, like many of my clients, felt that
the chaos of her childhood abuse was to be her destiny.

In this sense, the pain of recalling these memories for Jesse is consistent with Janet Reno's observation that such inner work always brings
forth 'the danger that the survivor may get nothing out of looking into
memories but more of the disorder he or she so dreads' (1990, 28), and
initially, at least, Jesse's recollections did appear to embody only chaos
and pain. For Jesse one particular memory of her father's incest supports this point.

This memory was brought forward in therapy notably later than
most others. It stood out for Jesse as more horrible than his other
assaults, because of the presence of her baby sister in the bed beside her.
In this instance Jesse's father performed oral sex on her.

I remember his face between my legs. I could not feel my body. I only
remember the bedroom light being on and my fear that the baby who was

in bed with me would awake. I could not look to see what he was doing to me. To this day I still can't look when something horrible is happening. I still remember that light.

Initially, her bringing this memory out of seclusion served little other purpose than to leave Jesse feeling deeply distressed. The image of the baby beside her during this incident of abuse reoccurred to Jesse repeatedly once she had spoken of it in therapy. The presence of the baby, who was her responsibility, had forced Jesse to remain aware of herself in that incident of abuse. She had not been able to disconnect herself as thoroughly from this act of incest as she had from her father's other violations of her. As a result she was forced to feel his violation more acutely and in all of her senses. The baby seemed to render Jesse's shame less private and her sense of vulnerability more intense by introducing this potential witness to what had always been a secret. In addition, the baby's role as unperceiving witness altered Jesse's own perspective on her abuse by setting up a comparison between the unviolated 'innocent' baby and herself.

After her body had been appropriated in childhood, the loss of her own sense of safety was felt more intensely than any of the other losses Jesse identified. This was typical in that a sense of loss is expressed in varying forms and degrees by most persons who have experienced disaster (Frankl 1959, 82). For Jesse the losses extended beyond her physical self to affect almost anything with which she had forged an emotional connection.

To illustrate, Jesse talked about some of the cruelties that happened around her. These were atrocities that she needed to voice as a way of releasing some of her own significant pain. One such incident involved her family's' rooster, that was left out in the cold and consequently lost a foot to frostbite. Jesse carried a deep sadness for the bird's neglect and suffering, which she finally expressed. 'I felt the rooster's pain as it hopped around the frozen yard pecking at grass seeds. I wasn't much better off than the rooster. It had no voice to say that it was hungry or cold and neither did I. I used to feel so sorry for it.' Jesse was able to empathize with the bird's neglect in a way that she initially could not do for herself. Her strong sense of hurt over the vulnerability and suffering of this rooster was, at the same time, a necessary expression of her own pain.

Telling the story released two other powerful memories of cruelty that had occurred when Jesse was still a young child. The grief that she demonstrated in therapy over these harsh and apparently senseless acts was so intense that her reaction clearly indicated an area for intensive work. Like her sexual abuse, these incidents were beyond her control to prevent. For Jesse, they symbolized a cruelty that was beyond expression. This is why we needed to uncover and give expression to their significance.

One story described the killing of her cat by a man who was drinking alcohol in the kitchen with her father. 'He had my cat in his lap. When hearing [the cat] purr a deep-throated purr, he told me that [the cat] was diseased. He then picked the cat up, carried him outside, wrapped it around a tree backwards until he snapped its neck and killed it.' Jesse sobbed as she relayed this story. She said that she wondered why she had to face this horror alone without anyone to protect her 'or the cat which I loved.' She added, 'I always loved animals so deeply.' It was significant for Jesse that in her recollection of this incident she had no memory of any intervention from an adult. Once again, she strongly identified with the animal's vulnerability. The second brutal killing, again of one of Jesse's pets, occurred again when she was a young child. She remembered 'an angry man running into our yard and chasing after my dog with a gun. He cornered him under our front porch where he shot and killed him. I heard the gun blast, a yelp, and then nothing. I was frozen to the spot. I can't remember what happened afterwards.'

These stories speak graphically of her powerlessness and the harsh environment in which she was forced to live emotionally and physically unprotected. Sharing these memories with me diffused some of her grief both through my absorption of it and my acknowledgement of its powerful effects on her. Importantly, the representation of these stories as metaphors for her own condition also prepared her to connect with her greater sense of loss: a disconnection from her body that her environment of neglect and exploitation had created. In preparation for this next step, then, she chose first to feel the losses that, while extremely painful to realize, were over time no longer quite so intimate.

Jesse's instinct, once disconnected for self-preservation, proved difficult to re-engage. As a result of her estranged relationship with her body, Jesse had frequently disregarded her most basic needs, including her need for physical safety from sexual violation, in favour of preserving the authority and dignity of those, mostly men, around her. This was a form of sacrifice, born out of objectification and fear that she had learned at a young age, beginning with her father's abuse of her. It had been necessary for her to comply with his regular attempts at sexual gratification, even though these dissolute acts violated her own sense of safety and dignity.

Jesse's emotional and physical levelling had been so completely effected that, in adulthood, her self-negation became embodied and internalized. The repetitive nature of the cruelties, exploitations, and pain that had been inflicted upon her and those she loved left her detesting herself and believing that she must deserve her fate. This sense of inevitability concerning her future caused Jesse to routinely jeopardize even her own most basic needs for physical safety. This cycle was, in part, what led to her repeated sexual victimization, well into adulthood.

Her sense of continued physical fear, coupled with a mistrust in her own capacity to defend herself, were pivotal issues in Jesse's decision to seek therapy. After intensive work Jesse began to establish a tentatively trusting reconnection with her body. She subsequently began to believe in her own capacity to protect herself. Yet in relation to this development she said, 'I have my body back now but not my head. I think that I can protect my body now, but my head hears things and goes places that I don't want it to.' When I asked where her head went, Jesse replied, 'Back to my childhood.' Jesse felt that while she had restored some semblance of control over her body, her mind was still being held captive by the abuse.

Control for Jesse had always been referenced upward. To seek it within herself then was a foreign venture. Yet gradually control began to signify looking inwards. In her search for more control over her 'mental images,' Jesse began to appreciate the insights gleaned from a close reconsideration of her own stories and memories. She started to actively and independently employ dreams in helping her to restructure her perception of her exploitations. Metaphoric expressions were most meaningful because they were her own to interpret, and consequently within her power to control and sustain. They were not externally imposed constructions or based on some system of expertise that was trying to create meaning for Jesse.

Jesse's abandonment of her search for an external explanation of her experience and an outwardly rendered recipe for her recovery represented a major turning point. In my practice, these metaphoric self-creations inevitably grow to become of paramount importance to the integration as they introduce the client to a trusting relationship with her own creative process. Jesse subsequently began trusting in her own capacity for producing the sustenance that she had been looking for outside of herself. The insights that Jesse gained in working through her sense of isolation and loss in turn stimulated her to redevelop a creative inner world. The perception of community that these parallels from popular self-help literature had once granted her were not forgotten but integrated into a more sophisticated and deeper understanding. In their original form they now offered little to sustain Jesse's pursuit of reintegration.

A Path of Reparation

Jesse's course of reparation in therapy was very much a continuation of her earlier inner development. Relaying dreams, locating metaphors, and telling stories drawn from her inner and outer experiences constituted the tools that Jesse employed for her reparation. As mentioned, reading too had provided Jesse an escape at a young age. Her earliest memory of being at peace was, for example, as a result of her strong identification with a character from a book. The freedom of fictional characters sometimes transported her for brief periods from her own violent environment into another. Through reading, Jesse had begun to nurture, within herself, what Joseph Chilton Pearce described as 'an inner scenario to replace the outer one' (1992, 168). The contents of this 'inner scenario' gave Jesse enough sustenance to surmount her usually fruitless outer environment.

During her recounting, Jesse had an occasional experience of what Denzin calls the 'relived epiphany.' This kind of epiphany provides profound insight into life's episodes, and 'meaning is given in the reliving of the experience' (1989, 71). Such revelations brought her to accept the fact that the powerless beings in her world – women, children and animals – were constantly brutalized. From this she realized further that she was not alone in her victimization and there was no innate flaw in her that invited the cruelty she was dealt.

While Jesse had been mostly powerless in the wake of her abuse and neglect, she had become strengthened and restored to a place of some prominence and control by independently transcending her former horrors and creating her own account of them. Her insights and newly discovered sources of strength sprang from what had formally been unimaginable locations. Yet they had needed to be discovered by her, carried forward, and given a prominent role. This demanded a creativity and self-reliance that could not be externally provided. It also represented a fundamental transition from a state of surviving into the more difficult work of survivorship.

As a result of having been sexualized and exploited intermittently throughout much of her life, Jesse was left disconnected from her body.

Ironically, she was acutely cognizant of herself as an embodied being because, from her earliest memories, it had been the focal point of her degradation and abuse. Existing in this perpetual state of perceived and real danger necessitated an unbroken vigilance (Woodman 1990, 133) in order for her to ward off further assaults. She lived in fear that this sort of degradation would reoccur.

The fact that her 'outer' environment continued to threaten Jesse in her adulthood was a source of chronic dread and enquiry for her. This important factor had stifled her ability to pass from victimization to some degree of self-authority. In effect, she had been stranded as a victim because she could not break the cycle of her abuse. Through therapy, she gained some comprehension of how, as a child, it had become possible for her to be so neglected and objectified, and yet not to have been at fault. Coming to understand why this pattern of cruelty and abuse repeated itself in her adult life, seemingly beyond her power to control, was a more difficult problem for her to resolve.

One revelation that contributed to freeing her from this cycle was Jesse's own conclusion that, despite forced submission as a child, she no longer had to submit to patriarchal authority and power. This comprehension triggered the breaking free from her 'victim' status, a status that she had come to consider as very much based on gender. As Jesse started to bear the responsibility for her own creation, through the narrative process, she recognized and came to value the strategies that she had employed as a child, and later, to cope with her chaotic environment. Jesse had thus independently caught a glimpse of her own power and creativity, which we then together nurtured.

One seemingly off-the-cuff statement stood out as a magnified moment and led to a breakthrough in Jesse's self-understanding and in my understanding of her. She said, 'If I came back in another life it would be as a hooker.' This striking comment seemed in apparent contradiction to Jesse's quest for a restoration of control. Yet she had apparently harboured this idea for quite some time before finding an arena where judgement was suspended and where it could be granted safe expression. The simple articulation of this thought carried with it a veritable flood of clarity.

Prior to this insight Jesse could make little sense of why she had chosen to pursue an extramarital relationship when she so strongly disapproved of her disloyalty to her husband. Nor could she make sense of why she continually craved and sought the affections of men, and 'needed' them to be sexually attracted to her when she abhorred their sexualization of her. These matters had, in a general sense, been discussed between us prior to this insight, but, as is most often the case, its full realization needed to be born of its own accord before another's theory could cast light upon it. Jesse's epiphany was the discovery that the nature of her relationships with men were, in part, a result of her attempts to redress the imbalance of power brought about by her father's and other men's sexual exploitations of her.

Newman's article exploring narrative, gender, and trauma presents a similar finding. The subject of her case study, like Jesse, was 'trapped in viewing her own sexuality and body from an objectified male perspective' (2004, 34). Through this revelation Jesse recognized that her physical desirability had become for her an important form of social power. She viewed men as being 'weak' in the face of her sexuality. Jesse saw hookers as engaged in 'a powerful occupation.' This reframing of her position, while a long way from complete, helped to restore to her some personal authority and remove her one more step from victim status.

One of the many complications stemming from the repeated violation of Jesse's body had been an undeveloped sense of her own capacity to create or achieve something that would be solely hers and would not be taken away from her. Her body, to use Newman's phrase (2004, 34), had become a 'social commodity.' On a strictly physical level, this was evident in Jesse's inability, in adulthood, to say no to unwanted sexual advances. For Jesse the thought of attempting to thwart such advances was intimidating, since she did not think she could tolerate the experience of what she perceived as another failure of self-defence. This feeling of powerlessness and acquiescence was generalized and carried over into other parts of Jesse's life. She felt that she could not own the reward of anything she produced. This feeling stemmed from her strong sense that she did not possess the being from which it emanated – herself. If she were successful, she thought, her accomplishments would be beyond her power to sustain.

One dream that Jesse relayed in therapy illuminated clearly her perceived lack of authority.

In this dream I am a child, yet I am an adult. I am walking along a path that is my path. My name is carved into it, like carving your name on a tree. It slopes down a hill and the trees have been cleared on both sides. It leads into a forest ... I discover that someone has destroyed my path and my name on it. I become terribly sad. I speak to a man I know and he says I can't have my own path. The dream ends with a dipping beacon light further along the path. It does not light up anything beyond it.

At the time she conveyed this dream in therapy, Jesse was aware that it held a special significance. The clarity and intensity of the meaning were consistent with the relived epiphany, and came retrospectively. She referred to the dream's path as symbolizing her life or herself and the liberties that men had taken with it. The defilement of this path was felt to represent not only the harm that had been done to her by her father and her other abusers, but her inability to reassert control over such violations. The man's denial of her right to have a path of her own represented also her current struggle with a lack of a sense of self-ownership. In all dimensions of her life, Jesse felt unable to assert a sense of possession. This previously unarticulated belief perpetually undermined any goal she dared to set for herself. Following this dream, Jesse said, 'I think of myself as never ever being able to make a decision about anything without having a feeling of dread.'

In our work with the dream's images Jesse remembered the man as someone from her community who had been greatly admired in their Pentecostal church for having memorized the entire Bible. When pressed for her further associations with this man, Jesse recalled that when he was younger, he had been 'terribly violent to his family.' The significance of these apparently contradictory descriptions, to Jesse, lay in their representation of a powerful conflict with which she had struggled daily: her father's violence and defilement of her and the church's patriarchic emphasis on purity and obedience. The influences that signified power for Jesse had almost always been produced externally to her and had, with few exceptions, been detrimental to her development.

That dipping beacon, which would not properly light her path, further emphasized this point. The way ahead was, symbolically speaking, in darkness. The beacon, like the church and her family, had held up the promise of illumination, protection, and enlightenment and had failed in these tasks. The power and sanctity promised by the church had not protected her from her father, either. Jesse recognized from this dream that if such promises were to be fulfilled, it would be up to her to make them happen. It was she who needed to light the path ahead. It was also becoming evident for Jesse, in conjunction with these insights, that such externally rendered constructions as 'survivor' would not provide the formula for her recovery. This too would have to be in her hands. These insights fuelled Jesse's struggle to locate an inner scenario to replace her bleak outer one. Yet the road was not straightforward.

She stated, with disturbing frequency, that every time she looked at her past, she saw and felt 'a heavy greyness.' And while she tried repeatedly to restore to herself some lightness of being, she experienced relief only in fleeting episodes.

Underlying Jesse's often debilitating depression there endured an intense fear of further exploitation by men. She seemed unable to break through her depression, for almost every early memory Jesse recalled contained some exploitative act or a threat of violence. The relief that she sought from the burden of these memories was eventually realized through acceptance of her narrative not as something to distance herself from. Instead, that same material needed to be integrated into a new working script. She then abandoned her efforts to return to an innocent pre-abuse self and began to focus on a new, more complex, and integrated self. The seemingly simple recognition of her abuse, as an ever-contributing source to her evolving narrative, represented, for Jesse, a personally transformative insight.

This breakthrough came for Jesse in the form of a dream that revealed a vital memory.

> I am walking in fresh vehicle tracks in snow. They are just wide enough for me to walk in. The track has one rut on each side with a flattened space in the snow in the middle but the track is wider than a car track. A car is coming face on. I am afraid for the safety of the girl child who is following behind me. I tell the child to go back. The child is impish, unafraid. The child stays just out of my reach but will not go back. I try several times to make her go back. I get angry with her but each time I look behind me she is still following me.

When asked for more details about the child and the dream, Jesse said that the girl struck her as 'unafraid, playful ... about four years old.' This image was striking to her. Jesse said that the child resembled her in her pre-abuse form, yet Jesse had no memory of herself as a child walking in vehicle tracks, since they did not have cars in her community until she was much older. (Many small Newfoundland outports were, and in some cases still remain, like Jesse's, accessible only by boat.)

Then she was struck by a clear memory of an uncle, whom she had been fond of, and she recognized the tracks in her dream as those made by his horse-drawn sleigh. This positive recollection from her past proved to be the link that Jesse needed to establish for her own reintegration. With the help of this dream she began to compile a series of memories that were comfortable to revisit. Jesse described this uncle as the only adult male she had ever loved and trusted. He would take Jesse and her cousins into the woods on his sleigh. 'He would put bells on the horses' necks and we would cut a Christmas tree.' By regenerating this relationship through dream and memory, Jesse was able to resurrect a capacity for trust and love that she thought had never been available to her. Without this dream, the memory of her uncle might well have lain dormant, unable to assist her.

A careful exploration of this relationship proved to be an important link to allowing trust to evolve in her present relationships. Like the bold child of her dream, Jesse had been free to be a child in the company of her uncle. 'It was safe to be a child with him and he was compassionate ... he felt for me.' Jesse went on to relay a memory involving her and this uncle that she described as 'both funny and sad.'

> My cousins and I snuck into an unfinished house that Uncle Joe was building. We were pretending we were grown-ups. We were smoking cigarettes that the older girls had been given by the American men from the forces base nearby. We were naked and pretending to be dressed like the older girls who wore long skirts with crinoline underneath and who dated the American men. We were pretending and smoking. We looked up from our play to see Uncle Joe laughing a big belly laugh at our childishness. He thought we were cute ... he was not perverted like my father and other uncles. We ran screaming when we were caught at our play. We were around nine years old.

Jesse sobbed, as she asked, 'Why couldn't my father have been like his brother?' This dream-memory combination was thus a catalyst in Jesse's reconstruction. It allowed her to mourn her losses and provided her with a foundation of hope on which to build her narrative. This uncle became larger than life in the remaking of her narrative, and it was necessary that he should figure so prominently, because he was to become her narrative's main symbol of love and understanding.

Jesse's relationship to her own account-construction highlights a general pattern that I have witnessed unfolding repeatedly. It begins, in the client, with an intense identification of an externally rendered description of her experience, epitomized by that of 'survivor,' and it leads to an eventual adoption of her own validity through the remaking of her story. Specifically, Jesse migrated from a stated sense of pride in her adopted survivor status to recognition that it was ill-suited for her.

Her perspective shifted from a burgeoning sense of dignity generated by her perceived inclusion in the wider group that the title implied, to a feeling of marginalization, rooted in an objectification that this label had also come to represent. The textually mediated description of 'survivor' had left little space for self-emanating constructions and reconstructions. Indeed, once the client's inner interpretative work has begun in earnest, its productions are in no way synonymous with mainstream interpretations. Jesse's process of integration required that we together delve into her unique storehouse of memories, reflections, and recreations in order for her to rediscover a personal sense of authenticity and a genuine belief in her own value. She needed to redo her story from the beginning to find guideposts that were substantial enough to exchange a fixed negative self-description for one that would continue to evolve constructively.

Fixed labels often produce a pre-valuation that is not necessarily accurate or captures only one strand of experience. The common attempt to fix a universal definition of self, in time and place, stands contrary to the reflexive quest for meaning and certainty undertaken by my clients. The socially fabricated label of 'survivor' places a border on their experience and limits their autonomy in this undertaking. In this vein Smith inadvertently captures the reflexive experience of client, therapist, and researcher and the interplay between the three, when she writes,

> The very forms of our oppression require a deliberate remaking of our relations with others and of these the relations of our knowledge must be key, for the dimensions of our oppression are only fully revealed in discoveries that go beyond what direct experience will teach us. But such a remaking cannot be prejudged, for in the very nature of the case we cannot know in advance what we will discover, what we will have to learn, and how it will be conceptualized. Remaking, in the context of intellectual enterprise, is itself a course of inquiry. (1987, 107)

As Smith suggests, client, therapist, and researcher alike must be informed about the web of influences that comprise the sources of our knowledge. For it is only in first being open to seeing them and then attempting to comprehend them that we can in turn begin to realize their influences upon us. Such openness to evaluating oppression also implies that these influences will be discerned only if we steer clear of fixed certainties and categorizations.

Accordingly, victims do not have to remain categorically fixed. As

Plummer suggests, 'Survivors can become post-survivors' (1995, 76). This observation highlights a hopeful direction for analysis derived from popular discourse. It promotes an ongoing evaluation the likes of which are cultivated in personal reconstructions, as opposed to opting for prefabricated self-definitions. In one way the semantic shift from 'victim' status to 'survivor' status indicates a step in the right direction. For one thing it has challenged the notion of blaming the victim. But the objectification nevertheless exists.

The outside movement of popular self-help literature, which offered a common language through which to describe sexual abuse, granted many of my clients the support they needed to instigate their recovery. This larger collective provided a kind of safety in numbers buffer, protecting against being swallowed up in a private humiliation and panic. Allying oneself with a larger group was for many a kind of safety valve. Yet as we have observed in the case of Jesse, 'survivor' status had its appeal until it was seen as an objectification of her and came to resemble the kinds of stigma with which she had grown up. In surrendering her private experience of abuse to a popular interpretation, Jesse found that she had once again given more of herself away than she could afford to part with. She then felt it necessary to distance herself from this imposed description and all that it stood for in order to create one of her own. That realization left her initially depressed and feeling once again betrayed by others. Gradually, however, she was strengthened by her discovery that she had some control over her own reconstruction and could remove herself from such objectification. Collectively, her personal metaphors fuelled reconstructions that steered her away from her previous search for a former, pre-abuse self and towards a new integrated sense of self drawn from past and present experience.

The process of change that many of my clients, including Jesse, have undergone to combat the residue of abuse they carry with them and the stagnant scripts that they have assumed is well summed up in the concept of reflexive transformation. As the next chapter shows, this process of stepping out of oneself to see oneself is in many ways an antidote to the objectification represented in the image of survival that is applied within the mainstream representations of sexual abuse. In an important sense, the building of each woman's account is a reaction to these popular constructions. They are attempts to define themselves in the face of a dominant representation of their experience. The antidote seems to lie in that part of each person's reconstructive process that was considered unique to the client herself. The images and metaphors that have arisen

in my clients' dreams and language, in the course of interacting symbolically, have certainly distanced us from the prevailing language and
its assumptions; they have granted the client a sense of authenticity and
sometimes a sense of ownership of her own interpretation. 'Survival,'
as this chapter has illustrated, is a static description when it is used only
to define or objectify those who have surmounted experiences of sexual
violation.

The course that most of my clients ultimately follow in order to transcend their abuse and their role as 'survivor' is better described as a
continuous cycle of transformation, with self-reflection at its centre. As
noted previously, Anthony Giddens was concerned with reflexivity in
the form of ceaseless revision of personal narratives in the light of a
significant social change. Alternatively, Barbara Myerhoff has concentrated on the intrapersonal experience of 'consciousness about being
conscious; thinking about thinking' (1992, 307) and the necessity of
translating this developing awareness to the outside world for a further
reflection of self. My clients' experiences, as Jesse's story indicates, and
as my next chapter further demonstrates, embody both of these elements of revision and self-consciousness.

3 Anguish, Dreams, and Remembering: The Reflexive Process

The previous chapter looked at one client's endeavour to repair and reconstruct herself and her resulting shift away from popular descriptions that claimed to define her exploitation. It also demonstrated that recovery, for the majority of my clients, had compelled them to become experts or authorities on themselves instead of uncritically accommodating to the elucidations of others. In their gradual efforts to piece together their experiences and develop their own understandings, they developed a sustained sense of mastery. For most, the depth and breadth of analysis necessary for recovery from such deeply ranging private damage required internal initiation. Yet while the content and character of each client's change needed to emanate from within, it was commonly the case that her previous marginalization and degradation also rendered her unable to recognize the necessary inner authority and creativity to begin this transformation alone.

Through the perspective of another client's experience this chapter extends the previous analysis by placing greater focus and emphasis on the nature of intrapersonal and reflexive therapeutic reworking. At points throughout this chapter, my presence as researcher and therapist is placed intentionally in the background. In these places I have chosen to allow my client's expressions and meanings to stand mostly alone. This approach spotlights her reflexive discoveries, which, as already noted, is something that we strive for in our exchanges. Typically, my therapeutic facilitation is more active in the early stages of contact and slowly retreats as the client claims greater command of her narration. This allows the direction of my client's path, from an intra- to a social reconnection to unfold. While in this chapter my research voice is more subdued than in the previous chapter, it exists nevertheless throughout in the structuring and presentation of this account and in the parts of the following narrative that I have chosen to omit or include.

When Dee was nineteen years old, she was gang-raped while at a party. In therapy her initial summary of the events leading up to the assault was sparse, unassimilated, and largely devoid of emotional content. Each new recitation incorporated more of Dee's feelings about the event, and more descriptive content was added with each subsequent telling. The few scanty details provided in the earliest descriptions included her becoming intoxicated, finding an empty bedroom in which to lie down, and then sending a friend to find her boyfriend. In a later, more detailed telling of her assault, Dee described herself awakening to find a man lying on top of her, sexually assaulting her. But Dee did not recognize initially what was happening. 'The room was dark,' and Dee thought that this man was her boyfriend. She said that she then became aware of someone near her head, holding it, and then 'sensed' that there were others in the room as well. She realized, 'through a fog of alcohol and sleep,' that the person having intercourse with her was a stranger and that she was being sexually assaulted. She then 'rolled herself into the corner of the bed and fell down into a space between the bed and the wall.' She added, 'I felt terrified.' In the aftermath of these assaults Dee experienced a kind of disintegration that is well summarized by James Carey:

> When tragedy strikes ... reality must be repaired for it consistently breaks down: people get lost physically and spiritually, experiments fail, evidence counter to the representation is produced, mental derangement sets in – all threats to our models of and for reality that lead to intense repair work. Finally, we must, with fear and regret, toss away our authoritative representations of reality and begin to build the world anew. (1989, 30)

Dee's sexual assault and its emotional aftermath had been internalized for so long that, to her, it had become inexpressible. To give words to this pain, if they could be found, would mean bringing to life all of the fears and disgrace that ironically had only become magnified during her silence. These private apprehensions included a dread of a social disclosure and judgement of her buried secrets. Contributing also to her silence was a growing belief that she was no longer a 'good' person, and that this assault had proved that she was 'dirty,' deserving this outcome. Because Dee could not readily understand and integrate her emotional and physical responses to this assault, she had an almost ever-present fear of 'going crazy.' She thus needed assistance in rendering her buried feelings into consciousness and endowing them with meaning. Or, as Carey says above, she needed to begin constructing her world anew.

Before Dee entered therapy, she dealt privately with the memory of her sexual assault by sublimation and minimization. In her view, the facts of her alcohol consumption and her lying down on a strange bed at a party left her blameworthy for the attack. Consequently, she avoided anything in her social world that might remind her of this violation, and she wanted neither to think nor to speak of it. Dee was unable to extricate herself and her experience from the negative cultural constructions that surrounded rape (Brownmiller 1975) or from her sense of self-blame for what had happened to her. The prospect of speaking to family or friends, let alone a therapist, about the assault carried with it the threat of having her worst view of herself confirmed or, worse still, of having this negative view verified by others. Thus, making conscious this experience, one that she had so actively and for so long tried to deny, was a threatening prospect. It registered as an apparently unbridgeable fissure that she felt unable to mend on her own. Yet she hoped that somehow in conveying her story she might eventually reconcile herself with it and thereby put an end to the self-blame and episodes of panic that suppressing it brought about. This desire and the sense that she could not achieve it alone motivated her to seek therapy.

Like Dee, many of my clients begin therapy with a strong sense that something needs to change quite substantially for them in order to rid themselves of the emotional pain and sense of degradation that they carry with them as a result of their sexual exploitations. Most come to recognize on their own accord that they need a fundamental reintegration. They appreciate too that they must perform this restoration if more personal, creative, and lasting solutions are to take root. As we saw in the previous chapter, clients often feel a strong initial inclination to reach outside of themselves, to find an alternative perspective from which to view their reality, and to find a remedy for their sense of self-fragmentation. But, as I have also argued previously, if the ideas or language of another are superimposed on her experience, the client will fail to develop the necessarily unique strategies for that reconstruction.

My clients have shared a common desire to locate an ally, in the form of a therapist, who would enter with them into their anguish and help alleviate the profound sense of social isolation that it has wrought. Each client thus commences therapy with a story that has been waiting to be told. Through the telling, these clients often hope to gain insight into how their sexual violation has consciously and unconsciously shaped and defined them in unsolicited ways. Generally speaking, they seek a release from the relentless grip of the abuse. Although most clients did not know what was in store for them when they entered therapy, many of them presuppose or perhaps only hope that the process to come will be positively transformative.

Retaining Contradictions

Therapy often begins with an exchange focused on engaging and drawing out the aspects of the client that were submerged as a result of their specific abuse. The desired conclusion of this process is to have the client locate enough personal substance to emotionally sustain her in initiating her own course of integration. One 'magnified moment' drawn from a dream or memory is sufficient to activate a client's reflexive process. Yet the source of the trigger that sets in motion this course of discovery ultimately cannot be planned or anticipated. Importantly, the dream or memory that reveals itself in this new way is also considered from a new perspective. Dee typified this process. Although she began her narrative with a guarded and surface relation of her assault, through her own account reconstruction and its resulting revelations she eventually developed and adopted a reflexive attitude. While the shift itself is not unique, the swiftness with which Dee opened herself up to her often terrifying, unconscious perceptions was unprecedented.

Dee undertook to suppress the reality of her violations for seven years before abruptly and aggressively attempting to integrate them. These were realms that she had decisively sealed off because any consciousness of them produced panic and fear. The process of making herself aware of her violations thus renewed in her conflicts and emotional extremes. It also prompted unsuccessful attempts to return to her previous state of unconsciousness. Herman offers a rationale for why these stories do eventually find some form of expression, despite the client's initial tendency to repress them:

> The ordinary response to atrocities is to banish them from consciousness. Certain violations of the social compact are too terrible to utter aloud: this is the meaning of the word *unspeakable*. Atrocities, however, refuse to be

buried. Equally as powerful as the desire to deny atrocities is the conviction that denial does not work. Folk wisdom is filled with ghosts who refuse to rest in their graves until their stories are told ... Remembering and telling the truth about terrible events are prerequisites both for the restoration of the social order and for the healing of individual victims. The conflict between the will to deny horrible events and the will to proclaim them aloud is the central dialectic of psychological trauma. (1992, 1)

Herman's schema of banishment, resurgence, remembering, and telling of a traumatic event describes perfectly Dee's response; it centres too on the individual/social integration that can occur. And, although she was initially unaware of it, Dee had entered therapy prepared to bridge these and other oppositions rather than have them further fragment her. During our therapeutic deliberations and external to them, she began to draw upon unconscious, symbolic, and metaphorical material, primarily in the form of dream content, in order to help her understand the horrific and dehumanizing experiences that had fragmented her. They helped her give voice to the depth of her inner struggle.

How does one make further sense of the resulting internal contradictions, and reinstate inner unity? Barbara Myerhoff's description of her own discovery of a reflexive perspective encapsulates perfectly the potentially unexpected sources from which profound and reflexive insights may spring. It demonstrates too how balance, reached through reflection, might be applied to internally and externally generated oppositions:

I witnessed a perfect reflection of the scene I inhabited in a still mountain lake that lay before me. So clear was the reflection that the two images were indistinguishable save that one was upside down. It was not necessary to choose between them. The image and reflection were fused, completing a reality between them, a totality that achieved a unification and state of perfection. Dream and waking life, unconscious and conscious, the above and the below, the hidden sacred domain and the palpable ordinary one were the same. The mending of those splits was a luminous experience that told me clearly, for the first time, why I had always been so attracted to and disturbed by the problem of reflected realities. (1992, 337–8)

Myerhoff's holistic vision of ostensibly competing realms becoming indistinguishably one was generated by her own reflexive gaze. In her uncompromising work with unconscious images, Dee, like Myerhoff, was later also able to produce a vision of unity that transcended her internal conflicts. What Myerhoff notes that Herman does not, however, is that the convergence of inner with outer realities can produce a reflexive condition that transcends mere survival.

Dee's problems were compounded by the fact that, following her assault, she began to experience symptoms ranging from panic attacks and indeterminate fear to a general mistrust of people. Sleeplessness, an inability to express sexual and emotional intimacy with her spouse, nightmares, a fear of being alone, and a growing tendency to detach herself from friends and her career were other signs of this self-disintegration. All of these escalating symptoms rooted in Dee's emotional reactions to her assault remained unexpressed for seven years. This secrecy increased her isolation and sense of incapacitation and heightened her fear of having her hidden life involuntarily revealed.

Dee's self-mistrust and her inner sense of fragmentation were made more complicated by a dimension of her story that remained concealed well into therapy. The disclosure of her assault in the protected confines of therapy had permitted her to develop a degree of trust. She consequently felt safe enough to disclose having undergone a pregnancy termination several years earlier, while living in an abusive relationship. Like the assault, the abortion had left her with a strong residue of guilt and an accompanying sense that she deserved the pain that she sus-' tained. Similar also to her sexual violation was the resulting all-pervasive fear of public exposure of the secret that it left her with. Prior to the assault, Dee had managed to cope with the abortion, mainly through an ongoing and deliberate effort to suppress the experience from her consciousness, which nevertheless failed, and to keep it a secret from others, including her husband and tightly knit family. This additional secret of her assault added an additional unbearable pressure, which she initially tried to deal with in much the same manner. However, taken together, these pains simply could not be suppressed. They began to seep out of her spontaneously and unwillingly in the form of anxiety attacks, social withdrawal, generalized fears, and nightmares.

Our most pressing initial therapeutic concern was that, in the wake of her assault and abortion, Dee was perilously alienated from her own body. The widening gulf between what she was actually feeling or not feeling, and the public persona she felt compelled to present, left her deeply split and, as mentioned, concealed a fear of 'going crazy.' These increasingly concentrated feelings had no obvious outlet prior to therapy, and as a result, an implosion of this harmful content seemed inevitable for her. While she readily identified her problems as stemming from her rape and abortion, she could not by herself locate a starting point from which to conduct any sort of reparation.

Yet for a client like Dee to feel immobilized in the face of such a deep personal fissure is not an uncommon reaction (Woodman 1990, 27). The disintegration of self that occurs following a sexual assault is always multilayered and thus formidable to those who must confront it. The impact of the damage brought about by such an assault affects the victim's conscious level – emotionally, mentally, and bodily – and transforms the unconscious level as well. Understandably, then, the client usually does not know how to advance with her reconstruction.

With sexual exploitation, a crucial faith has been betrayed. Such violations not only create intrapersonal fragmentation but also disrupt all relationships, since the very cornerstone of intimacy – trust – has been fundamentally injured. This breakdown of trust is an immediate issue facing client and therapist. To tackle this issue, before all others, has proven to be an effective therapeutic approach since the issue of trust, in some way, touches most of the other problems that will eventually face us. It represents a pivotal dichotomy between personal and social that equally concerns therapeutic and social research. My therapeutic work leaves me with little doubt that trust and the reflexive process are tightly interwoven where matters of sexual violation are concerned. Regrettably, the regeneration within the client of the capacity to trust is not simply a matter of an intellectual shift. The client's quest for reintegration necessitates that she get to the root of its breakdown by bridging an intrapersonal split that fosters mistrust at every level. The process of making conscious her unconscious reasons for her loss of trust, with all of its attendant emotional content, is what makes the reparative project so immensely complicated and indeed so necessarily reflexive.

Trust, Giddens writes, is the thing that 'generates the "leap into faith" which practical engagement demands' (1991, 3). Understanding the role of trust, then, is a way of facilitating clients' outward processes of reflexive transformation, as it is vital to the formation of intimate relationships (Seligman 1997, 18). A significant degree of trust must also develop between the client and the therapist within the therapeutic relationship, or the process fails. Moreover, a client's trust of another person, beginning with the therapist, represents her initial step toward the re-establishment of trust in general. Without a restored capacity for trust, Dee, for example, would have lacked intrapersonal continuity and remained isolated from others.

The most acute intrapersonal crisis of trust that occurs in the wake of the sexual assault experience is one that stems from the victim's sense of failure over not having protected herself from her injury (Herman 1992, 148). This loss of self-trust is less easily understood than the violation of trust that comes from being hurt by another. Whereas the client can typically justify and rationalize another's betrayal of her, she cannot or will not, initially at least, forgive herself. Such interpersonal fragmentation, as Dee's, commonly leaves the client initially powerless to trust her previous or existing perceptions or to accurately access and respond to current threats in her environment (Woodman 1990, 133).

For all of these reasons and more, the loss of trust in oneself is a difficult and complex gulf to bridge. An assault of the physical body frequently triggers a mind-body split commonly known as 'disassociation.' At one time disassociation was viewed strictly as a psychiatric malady. Now, it is also considered to be a 'survival' tool employed, mostly unconsciously, by those who have endured sexual abuse or other traumas. Herman summarizes the current understanding of this label while also lamenting its limitations in fully encapsulating and embracing the client's experience. She writes, 'Through the practice of dissociation, voluntary thought suppression, minimization, and sometimes outright denial, they learn to alter an unbearable reality. Ordinary psychological language does not have a name for this complex array of mental maneuvers, at once conscious and unconscious' (1992, 87).

This partial departure by the client, while protective to some extent, is also the ultimate violation of self-trust, for its unconscious components operate beyond the victim's control. Borrowing from George Orwell, Herman prefers to call disassociation 'doublethink' (1992, 87–8). It means 'the power of holding two contradictory beliefs in one's mind simultaneously, and accepting both of them' (87). I like Herman's adaptation of doublethink because it considers and confirms a spatial dichotomy that I have witnessed within my practice many times. Doublethink is a defence mechanism that isolates and, in part, shields the mind from the trauma that the body is undergoing. This separation allows the victim to exist in two places at once. It necessarily occurs both consciously and unconsciously. It also entails a fragmentation of the client's psyche from her body and a distancing from her immediate social environment. Doublethink, as I have observed it, distorts the client's capacity to describe her exploitation in a way that makes sense to others. Her experience appears illogical because it contradicts itself. Consequently, the client comes to view her relationship with herself and others with a deep and abiding mistrust.

In therapy, this split within the client and between her and others is exceedingly complicated and difficult to mend. To heal this rift requires a level of client insight that has most often never before been demanded of her. This must be closely worked with in therapy. As she begins to garner strength and insight from mostly internal sources, she also enters a period when external contacts seem untrustworthy and frequently hostile. This apparently contradictory reaction, the variance between opposite sources of self, produces an awareness that Myherhoff calls us to view as an enlightening aspect of reflexivity: 'Alienation and self-knowledge are tightly linked, if not causally connected, and reflection, introspection, hedonism, anomie, reflexiveness are all likely to occur under these conditions' (1992, 313). Somewhat ironically then, the beginning of self-trust takes the client in an initial direction contrary to what therapy intends to accomplish. Disintegration precedes individual and social integration. This process is helpful for, in a sense, it forces the client to look inward for solutions and from that perspective to then recognize life's seamless interconnectedness. Restoring a sense of self-sufficiency is a crucial first step in the reflexive reintegration of self.

Symbolically Conveying Experience

In her role as narrator and in the attempt to make conscious her unconscious processes, Dee used her dreams primarily to recreate and convey meaning. This component of reflexive therapy is what I seek to highlight in the following discussion. It marks the beginning of the client's search for more personally relevant forms of representation. It reflects what Giddens refers to as the 'emergence of an internally referential system of knowledge and power' (1991, 19). Such an emergence, as experienced by my clients, occurs when the old points of reference – a language and symbolism that were never their own – are replaced by ones that they have had a direct hand in generating.

To begin, because Dee was plagued by nightmares, we decided to scrutinize them. They offered a way of talking about Dee's fears, without triggering the anxiety that any mention of her rape, and to a lesser extent that her abortion, had produced. Dreams, and even nightmares, we discovered, were easier for her to probe than her waking fears and anxieties. Within those dreams that Dee identified as the most significant or transitional, we together located three recurring themes. Through the progression of our work with them, each series of dreams offered more in-depth associations. And we revisited these dream sequences frequently, since Dee used the metaphors in them to develop her understanding of her experience and to communicate an emerging identity to me.

The consistent metaphors that emerged in these sequences featured young children, dogs, and plant life. Dee considered that contact with all three of these living forms brought her, in her waking reality, closer to an emotional and physical lucidity that the assault and abortion combination had separated her from. Further, Dee identified each as important in her everyday experience. Unconsciously, however, she had some deeper and more troubling associations with these symbols. In their original form within her dreams, they were not entirely peaceful or welcoming. The plants were often dying or uprooted, dogs were frequently in need of protection from harsh elements, and the children were extremely vulnerable, if not in outright danger. She viewed all three life forms in general as dependent and in need of nurturing. All three metaphors signalled a distress that Dee had been attempting to conceal.

Concentrating on this child, plant, and dog series led to Dee's discovery that she could redevelop sensitivity to neglected dimensions of herself through communication with these entities in both their literal and symbolic forms. In fostering her capacity for nurturing, they directed her attention to the neglect and subjugation of herself following her assault. Her social retreat, designed to shield her from further humiliation and judgement, alienated Dee from all relationships except the three that recurred in her dreams. Yet when her dreams revealed that even these emotional relationships were increasingly tenuous, this became a signal to her that she was in danger of an almost complete withdrawal from dimensions of herself and from her social world.

Dee recognized that by continuing to pull away from the content of her own life, she was increasing an already widening intrapersonal split. The sense of optimism and mastery that this self-generated insight provided was unmatched by anything that Dee could extract from mainstream therapeutic and, more specifically, sexual-abuse-related literature. The major therapeutic advances that continued to grow out of her subsequent creative remaking took place only after Dee had placed herself at the centre of this process, when in her waking reality she had become its creator. She therefore had to allow those previously unbearable images to be made fully conscious and begin working with them in relation to the dream images that she was producing. She had to situate herself thus in the centre of her narrative in order to rightfully claim its authorship (see White and Epston 1990).

Within our therapeutic exchange, these dreams were researched until Dee located the 'right' meaning. When she could communicate her traumatic experiences through them, without compromising the power and meaning that the symbols held for her, she knew her analysis was accurate. The location of strong and local metaphors enabled Dee to voice what had seemed too vast, contradictory, and remote to communicate. They thus served as the foundation of Dee's reparation and ultimately provided her with comfort and regeneration. The ensuing sense of security she achieved was a release for Dee's creativity, which, in turn, permitted her to generate her own solutions and to remedy her personal and social disintegration. The task of therapy was then to provide a safe place for the translation of her dream symbols into a shared understanding of her experiences. The subsequent rendering of these experiences into a mutually navigable form then allowed her and me, in this relation of 'reflected realities,' to develop further insights. A prolific dreamer, Dee enthusiastically provided her dreams for our consideration. Discussed below, they are viewed here in relation to a series, which only later became evident. The order in which Dee's individual dreams presented themselves became a self-designed pathway of reconstruction and reparation.

The first dream she presented, the beginning of a series of related dreams, was a mere fragment containing symbols of plant life and a dog. Quite succinctly it addressed her feeling of disconnectedness as well as her manifold sense of loss: 'My young cousin had upset all my plants and destroyed them. Mom had forgotten to let my puppy back inside the house. I found the puppy frozen outside and became very upset.' As a 'presenting' dream in therapy, this one provided us with a sound general indication of Dee's condition. In it, the sobering and sad image of the frozen puppy conveyed to both of us Dee's present emotional state. She responded to this image with great emotion and related the image of her frozen puppy to her own sense of guilt, neglect, abandonment, and grief that arose from her rape. She viewed the destroyed plants as the current arrested state of her emotional and spiritual growth that was the result of her violation. Dee identified directly with the dream's subject of destruction and neglect. She did not believe that she could ever trust others again as she had done on the night of her sexual assault. It spoke too of her self-abandonment since her assault and, importantly, focused on Dee's need to resume control over her own care. Significantly it was her own symbols that first allowed Dee an open expression of her tremendous sadness. One is reminded that this function of authorship is pivotal for asserting authority and appropriating a language that women have had only a minor role in designing.

Upon relaying this dream fragment to me, Dee said that in her waking reality she cherished both her dog and her plants. She spoke of them as symbolizing 'the state of perfection that we are born into.' She defined her very close relationship to gardening in her waking world as experiences of 'bringing to life' and 'nurturing growth' within herself, for, despite the rape's splintering effect, Dee had retained an unsullied affection for young children, plants, and animals. Herman, in having observed a remarkably similar tendency among her clientele, suggests, 'The patient's own capacity to feel compassion for animals or children, even at a distance, may be the fragile beginning of compassion for herself' (1992, 194).

As the client attempts to integrate her disparate components following sexual assault, she begins to understand the full impact of the multifaceted 'split' that has taken place. In particular, the assault and its accompanying psychological rift result in her feeling alienated not only from her relationship with her own body but from the language she has traditionally employed – a symbolic link to her social and cultural world. Many clients discover that their own language has become inadequate to describe their experience, so they look outside for meaning. This recognition corresponds to Smith's notion of 'borrowed language' (1987, 4). It suggests the idea that the means used by women to reflect upon themselves thus often becomes a reflection from outside of themselves (52). My clients' attempts to relay their extreme and emotionally complex experiences repeatedly demonstrate the deficiency of the language. Thus, if they do not assemble their own meaning, their stories will invariably reinforce feelings of negation and isolation.

The lengthy dream that follows illustrates an early attempt by Dee to reintegrate fragmented parts of her self, and in so doing, to locate a language supported by her own symbols that was powerful enough to absorb and express her experiences.

I was in a large field with some other people. I saw a lady running in the field, crying because she couldn't find her puppy. Myself and this other person both look to the side in a swampy area. The rest of the people were looking in the field. This other person went into the swampy area first. I then followed and retrieved the puppy. The puppy was very limp. The lady started crying again (thinking the puppy was dead). I put my mouth over the puppy's nose and mouth – then started to blow air into his lungs. The puppy began to move shortly afterwards. He was alive ... Dream switched a little ... I was in the same area but now it was a baby frog in my mouth ... with like a bubble being blown out ... this was the only part you could see. There was one other person (female) with me. I was determined to save this animal but I needed help. I was unable to speak as the frog was in my mouth. So I used hand and facial expressions to get the importance of this animal's survival across to other people. Sometimes this other person would talk on my behalf if they really did not get my point. I was travelling and talking with people trying to find this one person who would understand and help/or trying to get my point across to different people I met. We finally arrived at this lady's office (she had a lot of power). We asked her secretary but she would not allow us to see her. She did not think it was very important. We happened to see this lady in one of the halls of the building and I was trying to speak using facial expressions ... She understood right away. She was very supportive to our cause. This lady became very angry with her secretary for not allowing us to see her. The secretary came into the office later with two papers with graphs on them in colour. The powerful lady was planning out everything to do to save this animal.

This dream demonstrates generally the reflexive nature of my clients' reconstructions. Significantly, it also illustrates the extent to which these transformations are often life-defining. Upon telling me this dream, Dee's first reaction to its content was to say, 'Frogs are awful and so is what I have to tell but am not expressing.' She also realized from this dream that she considered me, as therapist, to be acting as her interpreter. In effect, the meaning of her account was translated, through me, as she acted it out. Dee's search for a means of expression was vital: like the elderly population of Myerhoff's study, it was a search for meaning and a new life.

In her prior dream, the puppy's death was beyond her control. Now, Dee was in command of the rehabilitation. Saving the vulnerable animal of this dream represented her ongoing quest to rescue what was vulnerable and endangered in her own life. Dee felt, for instance, that her instinct for self-preservation had failed her during and after the assault. This produced a strong mistrust of herself. Since animals operate on the level of instinct, this dream rescue was, in one sense, about saving her instincts. A concern with her own perceived failed instincts was evident in she questions she posed repeatedly: 'How come I was not protected? How come I could not protect myself?' The dream also raised an important question: was speaking about the horrible event a means to her reintegration? The metaphors in this dream certainly suggested that it was. By speaking, the dream suggested that Dee could rescue the unconscious puppy, her own instinct.

Through this dream Dee was able to communicate to me what she needed my role to be in her integration, even to completely formulate the idea or find the words to express this need. Through the dream she asserted control over the direction of her reparation before fully recognizing the need to do so or realizing that she could even achieve this goal. It contained her self-designed prescription for recovery and was presented in a form that was clear to us both.

Moreover, her perception of having found a 'powerful interpreter' augured well for the establishment of trust between us. Finally, this dream indicated to us both that she must begin taking the lead in the therapeutic dialogue and, in so doing, exercise more fully her own forms of expression.

Importantly, Dee had now discovered an environment where she felt safe and understood. She had additionally found a language that made it possible to satisfactorily express her experience. The dream suggested too that she had already inwardly found the solution she had been seeking. It was not the therapist, but rather she who was most responsible for the resuscitation of her identity and for the guardianship of its vulnerable and intuitive dimensions. I, as therapist, merely facilitated her expression of that newly emerging self through a language that both of us could understand, but that only she could possess and develop.

Ascertaining Inner Authority

Victor Turner's description of nineteenth-century writer Henry David Thoreau's reflexive transcription with himself typifies my clients' processes once they finally locate inner authority:

> He was an animal nourished by a crop he was cultivating, which was both an example and a symbol (a use and a mention) of the process of cultivation by which the human race became human; he was a writer whose met-

aphorical language cultivated his physical activities and rendered matter into meaning; and he was a critic of language who enjoyed pointing out how his own tropes both expressed and exemplified the process of self-cultivation he had embarked on. (Turner and Bruner 1986, 74)

As Turner suggests, the cultivation and application of symbolism is central to the success of self-reflection. My clients regularly find nourishment and growth in the living symbols and metaphors that they call upon to contain and lend meaning to their own experiences of self-cultivation. And, similar to Turner's interpretation of Thoreau's experience, the pursuit of meaning and realignment of self needed to be privately nurtured before the narrative was turned outwards in search of further self-reflection.

As mentioned previously, Reno too surveyed the apparently innate and universal human need to create symbols and metaphors in order to 'recover psychic and emotional wholeness' (1990, 21). Reno's focus, however, does not remain with the socially isolated component of recovery. The experience of the individual and the importance of symbolic location as a means of self-explanation and recreation are inextricably linked to the social. And it is through a conduit such as the narrative, as process, that this experience is related to an audience, and in the act of relating is thus transformed. Her analysis of Ishmael, as a metaphor for the survivor's plight and the surpassing of trauma, resembles closely the tangible experience of my clients. By probing *Moby-Dick*, as a symbolic and ultimately social process, she brings to the fore the phenomena that I have observed in my practice.

> Though it is painful to confront the specter of one's guilt, it is necessary to do so in the process of achieving wholeness. Wholeness for the survivor means reintegration into the human universe, and this is the aim of the survivor's narrative. In reliving the disaster through telling it, the survivor may arrive at metaphors and symbols suitably encompassing for his or her needs, so that he or she may fully participate in living again. (Reno 1990, 28)

Another of Dee's dreams illustrates with immediacy this simultaneously individual and social integrative process of initiating change that these authors analyse. The metaphors she appropriated took her one step closer to the inexpressible content that she felt she had to integrate yet from which she had previously disassociated, for through this dream, the initial fear stemming from her abortion and assault was acutely revived.

The house in her dream symbolized Dee herself, in which she opens multiple doors – or aspects of herself – that previously had been unseen and un-entered. Just like the secrets that she had been concealing, some of these rooms never seen before were dark and frightening.

> I was in our house and cleaning the rec. room. While I was doing this, I rediscovered an area of the house not used. There was a large round bar with a large storage space behind it (area light). [To get to] this area, I went down a couple of steps. I then went down a few more steps that led to a basement area: dark (very dark). To my left was a bedroom, to my right was a bathroom – very pretty and bright (looked brand new). On the same side was another bedroom. I was very afraid as soon as I entered. I could feel an evil presence. I left and ran back upstairs. [My grandfather] visited and wanted to see our house. I showed him around. When we got to the two bedrooms downstairs, he thought I should have my seedlings in the room to my left. I did so while he was there (maybe because he has a green thumb). I did not show him the room on the right ... I did not feel scared at this point. I thought after he left that I should move the plants back upstairs. They would not get enough light to grow down there. Mom and Nan visited after. I showed them the house. I remember being very upset and scared when we neared the room. They said how pretty the bathroom downstairs was, not saying much about the two rooms (I once again could feel the presence of something evil when we entered the [other] room). It was so dark I was unable to see anything. It was cool and damp feeling. When we went back upstairs, I got the feeling that the two rooms should be redone and much lighter. [My husband] came home a little later. I told him about the other room and how I felt. He looked around and I went with him. He said that he did not notice anything. I voiced my concern over my seedlings and he helped me bring up a few trays. I felt terrified while we were downstairs, looking towards the second room. I had three trays left to bring up. [My husband] did not want to go back down again. The dream turned a little. I think we were in a mall. I was there with a friend talking when I saw [my husband] talking with this lady. She owed him ten dollars which he wanted in two dollar bills only. As he took the money they were standing very close. [He] then left. Then I saw you (Marie) talking with some people about their problems. You asked me to join the group. I asked to speak with you alone. I told you about the new parts of the house that I had found and about the room on the right. You

understood fully. I remember telling you things such as how I was going to get the three trays out one at a time by putting one on top of the other. I wondered if I could lift the weight.

When I asked Dee what she believed the dark rooms represented, she readily identified them with her abortion and sexual assault. The presence of evil she discovered in her dream's two rooms was concentrated enough to be a worthy representation of the power that these two events had grown to assume in her shame and silence. In response to my inquiry about what she might need in order to metaphorically enter those rooms, Dee's unequivocal response was 'light.' She said that light, in this context, meant insight into her experience. Light also represented Dee's need to release her secrets from their symbolic darkness and, by externalizing them, break the hold that they had on her.

Also, Dee readily understood this dream as a message that it was up to her to provide the necessary 'light' or insight for her sustenance. She recognized that, like the seedlings she urgently wanted to remove from that dark place, she was not thriving. Identification with the seedlings removed much of Dee's shame by distinguishing her current condition not as a personal failure, but as a product of existing in an environment that had been fundamentally deficient. Figures central to her survival had been negligent and abusive. She surmised from this conclusion that no one, other than she, could assume responsibility for her own insights or her own survival. In the language of her dream, Dee saw that it was ultimately up to her to illuminate the dark recesses represented by her unintegrated negative experiences. She understood accordingly that by making them conscious they could constructively alter the direction of her account.

Dee's next dream positioned her one step closer to facing her fears and thereby altering the outcome of her own account. As the dream's images illustrate, however, making previously unconscious material conscious can be a threatening task.

I was riding Skidoo with another person. We were at the top of the mountains. We came to a place where the mountain dropped off. On the next mountain, which was very close, there were two large chains. The chains were there in case anybody went over the cliff. We were doing this for fun, driving over the edge, holding on to the chain and coming back to the top. It was my friend's turn again. When the chain was taken hold of some ice broke away from the chain and this person fell to their death. I noticed this

man who was set free from the ice. This was a very evil man. I noticed he
was trying to get my dog at the top of the mountain. I was angry and
fought this person to keep him away from my dog. I was on the other end
of this chain trying to get to top of the mountain first. I got Jo Jo and threw
her to Mom and Dad. They got her and drove off. She was safe. That evil
man couldn't reach her anymore.

Our reflexive analysis of this dream revealed that the fears that Dee had
been unwilling or unprepared to confront were released from the frozen past in an 'evil' form. The friend or ally symbol falls to her death
while playing with the mechanisms that were set in place strictly for
their safety. Dee's interpretation of this sequence was important. She
viewed the 'friend' as that dimension of herself that had distracted her
in her own life, from the important task of facing the assault and abortion and from integrating the emotional repercussions of the two
events. While this 'distraction' had once provided her with necessary
protection from a potentially overwhelming reality, it now prevented
her from addressing an important contradiction in her story. In effect
her silence, which had once been perceived as protective, was now
undermining her safety and reparation. This approach had ultimately
jeopardized her by cutting her off from several fundamental dimensions of her experience and herself, and eventually from her social network. Nevertheless the dream proffers a transformative metaphor. Dee
does pass her dog (instincts) to safety and experiences anger at having
been thus threatened.

In our subsequent analysis of the dream, the personal agency that
this forceful response signified was not lost on Dee. The metaphors
reflected that while her fear was intense, her willingness to be more
assertive was also burgeoning significantly. Dee now realized that if she
continued to suppress the negative features of her experiences by denying their relationship to her, she would remain splintered and isolated
and thereby ill-equipped to manage her reparation. She further understood that additional personal strength and insight might develop from
an incorporation of those experiences. Her changed approach consequently involved a direct confrontation of the memories that had been
holding her hostage and had separated her from her own spontaneity
and self-guardianship. In effect, this dream had given Dee profound
insights into matters that, until then, she had not yet fully appreciated.

Like the fear of the darkness in those basement rooms or the evil man
emerging from the ice, images of what Dee called 'evil' plagued the

dreams that followed her assault. But evil was also a waking preoccupation. She had grown increasingly afraid of her own and other people's capacity for evil. Because Dee had adopted and internalized the blame for her rape and abortion, she had come to view both of these acts as 'evil' (Ricoeur 1967, 33) components of herself. But in opening herself up to her 'dark' secrets, Dee did much to alter her state of guilt. Herman's description of what often then happens is consistent with my observations: 'The reward of mourning is realized as the survivor sheds her evil, stigmatized identity and dares to hope for new relationships in which she no longer has anything to hide' (1992, 194). The symbolic deaths in her dreams facilitated Dee's mourning the loss of her stigmatized identity. Their symbolic manifestations marked this passing powerfully. As a result she began to feel less like the embodiment of the evil that had been acted out upon her.

The next dream fragment moved beyond Dee's preoccupation with evil to illustrate her growing self-assurance, as constituted by potent internal representations of her authority: 'I was trying to baptize a small boy who was in emotional pain. He was hiding under the red cloth of the Baptismal, afraid to come out. I was trying to get him to emerge. He was frightened. I exorcized him.' Dee viewed this boy as representative of her own besiegement and distress. Like the child, she had been terrified, hiding, and hoping that her protection and salvation would somehow be mystically enacted. Now, even in the presence of such fear, Dee attempted to take command of her fears through a symbolic exorcism and to expunge the hold that they had on her. Her dream's expression of compassion for the hiding child permitted Dee to recognize and understand her own impulse to retreat from her fears, and this prepared her to sympathetically confront them.

Dee's subsequent dreams continued to be vivid and prolific. They touched for her an 'authentic' core located beyond her reach after her assault. Metaphors in these dreams enjoined Dee's experience where straightforward description failed. Then, as she continued to revive self-trust through her own images, and to remember and mourn for her former self, the evil surrounding her became less gripping and prepossessing. Through her narrative that was fuelled and substantiated by these images, Dee eventually constructed for herself an energy and enthusiasm for living that she had not felt since her sexual violation. In addition, these dreams provided her with symbols and metaphors at once personal and universal, which aided in uniting what had been an ever-widening chasm between her personal troubles and her public self

(Mills 1959, 8). This merging of the internal and external self was a necessary part of her overall reintegration.

Like all of my clients, Dee needed to clarify and make communicable what had happened to her, through a personally relevant language. Otherwise this transmission would not have been faithful to her experience and could not, then, have been restorative. Coming to this recognition and locating means to carry it out constitute the work of the initial stages of the therapeutic process.

As a consequence of this work in the early stages of therapy, Dee's initial vulnerability and grief transformed into a stated anger over what had happened to her. Again, her consciousness and communication of this inner change was brought to light through a dream.

> I was walking around [my brother-in-law's] new house under construction. His grandfather wanted me to help with the pouring of the basement ... wanting me to assist him making a grid made of string to pour the floor evenly. I had found my laundry hamper (empty) and a basket of clean clothes folded. I was bringing this over to our house when grandfather [in-law] asked for help. I was going to return as soon as I brought over the clothes. As I was walking over the grass I noticed a man moving my trees. I flipped (very, very mad). I knew it was my father-in-law who had ordered these things to be done. One tree was moved to the side a little more. This tree is near the front garden anyway. I could live with that more but wondered if he had the hole big enough for the root ball. Could the tree grow well or survive? The other tree was moved from the side of the house to the front garden. The crane had just finished digging the hole and was getting ready to put the tree in. I was savage. I grabbed the tree and planted it where it should be. I also noticed that he did not have the hole big enough. I wondered if the other [tree] would survive. I then looked and he was putting topsoil over the lawn (front), going to level it out. I was outraged. Where does he get off doing what he felt, without even asking.

Dee later regarded this dream's theme of transplantation as transitional in her reparation. The image of invasive and involuntary uprooting, and her associated rage, was reminiscent of the sense of violation she had experienced following her sexual assault. Yet the anger associated with that event came to life first through this dream. That experience of bodily violation had uprooted her from her own groundwork, had upset her sense of equilibrium, and had disrupted her capacity for self-nurturing. Recognition of these things had not been expressed then, if indeed it had been perceived. Nevertheless, Dee's image of her angry demand, that she do the transplanting herself, spoke to her of the necessity of now taking command and once again rooting herself.

Using such dream metaphors as a personal guide, Dee began to manage her own reintegration. Again, as with the more fragile plants and seedlings of earlier dreams, the job of transplantation had to be done by Dee herself if their (her) survival was to be ensured. The metaphor of the transplantation of much hardier trees, however, posed another significant meaning, that she had grown heartier and less vulnerable. Accordingly, it was now safe for her to be angry. The anger expressed in the 'uprooting' dream proved both energizing and appropriate. It indicated too that an eventual synthesis of her fragmented self would not come from compartmentalizing or refuting any part of her experience but from making it, and the emotions associated with it, conscious and then giving them expression.

Self-Regulating Reintegration

Like the presentation of stories in Myerhoff's study, Dee's dreams arose and were expressed spontaneously. Their significance often became clear through the process of communication itself. As Myerhoff noted of her subjects, 'Self-interpretation came into being as it was formulated. It did not exist clearly or in a coherent fashion until it had been publicly demonstrated' (1992, 340). With the telling of each dream, and the succeeding reflections they received, Dee became a stronger and more proficient interpreter.

The next dream, the last of Dee's 'dog' series to be discussed here, is one that Dee identified at its conception as important. While most of her dreams were left untitled, this one she named.

I had a very in-depth dream. [My former boyfriend] was after me. [My husband] and myself had left [my former boyfriend's] house. He followed us outside into the driveway. [My husband] was in our car and I was guiding him out of the driveway when [my former boyfriend] hit the side of our car with his car. I was scared sitting down on the driveway. [My former boyfriend] threw some things at me and [my dog] was one. I grabbed [her], holding her close. I ran away ([my husband] was gone also) ... I was inside another house with three to four other women ... I was a little older. We were all sitting on the stairs at different levels. Below me was a young girl crying with her head in the lap of another woman a step ahead. (This young girl was me who had just run away from [my former boyfriend's]. I was sitting above all of them with [my dog] in my lap looking down over them understanding all the pain ... I was in the hospital visiting some people. Mom was one of them. She was sitting in a wheelchair crippled on one side (arm bent up, very thin looking, unhappy). [My former boyfriend] was somehow related to her state.

Dee commented on this dream in a note that followed its entry in her journal. 'I call the above dream *Starting Over*. I had escaped from my past and had gained understanding of it ... looking down on people trapped in the same kind of pain, knowing it could have been me without any understanding.'

In our next session, Dee further explicated this dream. According to Dee, these figures represented stages in her development. With reference to her mother's role, Dee felt that her mother had been supportive to the point of emotionally carrying her, and that she had identified with Dee's pain. Yet she had not been a part of her daughter's most recent evolution. Dee also understood that she had reached insights about herself that neither her mother nor anybody else had been able to provide or could fully understand. This awareness represented a transition that was both painful and liberating. The letting go of her traditional dependency, symbolized by her mother, was frightening to her. Yet Dee realized with the help of this same dream that she was now emotionally free from the abusive relationship with her former boyfriend and all that it represented to her. She had symbolically left him, and she had taken with her, in the symbol of her dog, her self-determination and her instinct for self-preservation.

Prior to entering therapy, Dee had dealt with her hurt and fears by operating on a peripheral plane only. She had disallowed her own interiority. This approach served a double function of keeping an awareness of her trauma at a distance and protecting her 'secrets' from unwanted invasions by others. In the short term, Dee's strategy of closing off parts of her history was effective for shielding her from haunting memories. But this strategy proved to be an ineffective coping mechanism when she became emotionally immobilized. Dee's fear of going 'crazy' indicated that she no longer held a firm sense of who she was 'unmasked.' The many facades that were necessary in order to conceal her secrets from herself and others had made her a stranger to herself.

The need and value of self-regulated reparation grew more apparent for Dee as time went on. She had always been a prolific dreamer, and she had become increasingly aware of the content and value of her dreams. In the course of her gradual communication of them to me, Dee restored to herself a belief in her own self-worth by reflexively reconnecting to dimensions of herself that had been repressed or denied and having those dimensions mirrored back to her. Further, by opening herself to the content of her unconscious, her understanding of what had happened became more authentic. In gaining this sense of authenticity and a fuller reconnection to her past, Dee learned to appreciate what Victor Frankl has expressed so well. 'Having been is also a kind of being and perhaps the surest kind' (1959, 90). More specifically, through the incorporation of her unconscious content into her waking script, Dee was able to restore to herself a firm sense of embodiment and greater self-integration.

The act of peering into a submerged world, regardless of the fact that it was her creation, was initially 'terrifying.' Her pronounced fear stemmed, in part, from a state of alienation from her other dimensions of self (see Burkitt 1999, 21). This, in turn, rendered that territory foreign and threatening. So as we have seen, Dee's dream metaphors included images of 'evil.' Through an application of these images to understanding herself, she came to terms with her own capacity for creating what were to her 'terrifying' symbols. To her relief, in talking about 'darkness' in symbolic form, Dee discovered that she had not brought more of this evil upon herself. And in recognizing her own capacity for constructing metaphors and symbols of evil she became less afraid of its social manifestations. Her dreams therefore provided her with a language complex enough to give meaning to her social world. Further, these metaphors did not trivialize her intense and personal experiences, as mere words or disembodied theorizing might have done. Gradually, her understandings of past events that re-emerged in symbolic form came to be viewed by Dee as personally accessible sources of clarity, creativity, and power.

The process I have described was not confined to intrapersonal analysis. Rather it reached beyond to include Dee's therapeutic relationship and social environment. In and through her dreams Dee located a seamless self with internal and external, dark and light, and bodied and disembodied dimensions all working as one. If not, it would not have been a genuinely reflexive endeavour. As Myerhoff points out, 'Reflexiveness does not leave the subject lost in its own concerns; it pulls one toward the other and away from isolated attentiveness toward oneself. Reflexiveness requires subject and object, breaking the thrall of self-concern by its very drive towards self-knowledge that inevitably takes into account a surrounding world of events, people, and place' (1992, 313). This is what happened to Dee as well as many of my other clients. Their reflexive processes provided associations from their internal worlds to their interpersonal environments, and as well to their social ones.

My practice demonstrates that this not necessarily linear progression strongly motivates the client's telling of her story. Frankl noted that 'the true meaning of life is to be discovered in the world rather than within Man or his own psyche, as though it were a closed system ... being human always points, and is directed, to something, or someone, other than oneself – be it meaning to fulfil or another human being to encounter' (1959, 115). Dee's narrative production demonstrates and affirms this outward gaze. But it is not a unidirectional process. Even so, her account shows just how internally rendered and focused reparations lead to a reconciliation of an isolated self with the broader human experience.

In her discussion of Jungian dream analysis and its application to sexual-abuse therapy, Bonnell Lewis Strictling says, 'What the client needs is some new point of view, something outside the ego's interests, analyses, and expectations, to provide fresh insight into and energy for struggling with whatever has brought her to therapy' (1990, 148). My client's symbols were the avenue through which fresh insights became available to us both. They prevented us from retreating into formulaic therapeutic approaches by keeping a fresh, intrapersonally meaningful resource ever before us. In addition to symbol work, in adopting the standpoint of sociologist and distancing myself from the mainstream sexual-abuse theories, I was enabled in locating fresh insights over and above my clients' own ones. I carried over to their experiences, and my understanding of their situations, the insights of another discipline.

4 From Silence to Narration: Exposing and Interpreting a Fragmented Self

The last chapter closed with Victor Frankl's reflection, substantiated by my clients' accounts, that being does not exist strictly within our psyches. It is interdependent upon meanings and relationships that we locate and create inside and outside of ourselves. This chapter expands that discussion and looks past the intrapersonal reflexive experience by examining one client who with great difficulty brought herself to speak and relay her account in therapy. Her perspective clarifies for us the value of narration itself as distinct from its specific content.

The power and worth of the narrative, as medium, for helping to define and express our life experiences is certainly not limited to the individual or to the personal, but extends to our shared collective consciousness of the world. In noting the power of the story, Plummer too comments upon its mounting importance within the social sciences:

> The ceaseless nature of story telling in all its forms in all societies has come to be increasing recognized. We are, it seems, *homo narrans*: humankind the narrators and story tellers. Society itself may be seen as a textured but seamless web of stories emerging everywhere through interaction: holding people together, pulling people apart, making societies work. Recently, from all kinds of different theoretical perspectives in the human studies – the folklorist, the oral historian, the semiotician, the anthropologist, the political scientist, the psychoanalyst – there has been a convergence on the power of the metaphor of the story. It has been recognized as one of the central roots we have into the continuing quest for understanding human meaning. (1995, 5)

As Plummer and others have said, giving expression to our internal phenomenon is vital. Yet this presumes that people naturally want to tell their stories.

But what of a client's silence? Given that many clients are spontaneously attracted to the power of their own stories, what does resistance to the narration of sexual-exploitation accounts tell us about the reciprocal relationship between the individual and the broader culture? In pursuing this inquiry, I look at how my clients express their sexual stories, what holds them back, and why they choose their particular audience, the therapeutic one, to hear their abuse narratives, for many of my clients agonize over lost memories or forgotten details because they think, and have indeed been told, that these ruptures in continuity detract from the credibility of their stories. Thus, how the account comes to be relayed is frequently related to the client's perception of the validity of her experience and, at least as important, her concerns that she be believed or might not be believed. While internally rooted, this insecurity is profoundly influenced.

In addition, I am also interested in how a client's ideas about herself are formed and exposed through these sometimes halting accounts, for fragments of memory, or even conflicting memories, if recognized and accepted by the client as an authentic way of recalling, assist her emotionally and intellectually in disowning the dominant verdict on her experience. Understanding her own methods of recollection and expression makes it possible for a client to trust an internal rendering and, in so doing, establish a sense of self-worth. These matters constitute the principal focus of the following narrative and its discussion.

In terms of *how* the account is constructed, my experience as a practitioner has consistently confirmed that stories are not recalled and relayed in a linear fashion. By way of illustration, Judith Herman's following observation is one to which I have often born witness:

> People who have survived atrocities often tell their stories in a highly emotional, contradictory, and fragmented manner which undermines their credibility and thereby serves the twin imperatives of truth-telling and secrecy. When the truth is finally recognized, survivors can begin their recovery. But far too often secrecy prevails, and the story of the traumatic event surfaces not as a verbal narrative but as a symptom. (Herman 1992, 1)

As an antidote to secrecy and the symptoms generated by silence, effective reflexive therapy provides an avenue for advancing in the client a belief in the validity of her perceptions and respect for her own ways of knowing and telling. Instead of regarding a client's fragmented memories as unreliable and in order to transcend her negative self-concept, we work with her to locate what is valid for her, thereby effecting a forward movement in her reparation. This approach can also transform the client's view of her 'symptoms' from that of problem to that of a catalyst in devising resourceful solutions for helping herself (White and Epston, 1990).

Wordless Expressions: Lauren's Account

It had been Lauren's choice to enter therapy. This was not a decision that her family supported, so she came at first without their knowledge. Her weekly return to my office signalled that she wished to communicate her abuse to me, yet she remained completely silent about it. Lauren knew that it was time to bring her experiences out of silence and this is why she had sought therapy. As it had for other clients, silence had served her as an important form of social protection, yet as negative symptoms came to dominate, it had lost its value. This recognition remained dormant for months while Lauren kept her therapy sessions yet said nothing about her abuse.

Silence in therapy can speak volumes. Lauren's silence, for instance, was part of her abuse. Like her sexually appropriated body, her attempts at articulation had been repeatedly negated. Peggy Penn describes how

> 'voice' [is] a useful metaphor for describing a social constructionist therapy that emphasizes language and voice. We have all worked with clients who cannot speak of traumatic events, whose voices were indeed 'lost', not because of resistance or withholding, but because the particular voice that needed to speak of the traumatic event could not be found or accepted. (1998, 300)

Consistently, external contestations greeted Lauren's attempts to tell her story. Past efforts to articulate her violations had consistently brought her physical and psychological punishment and humiliation. This complicated her integration of these events and served only to have Lauren turn this rejection in upon her self. Because her silence was not only constructed but supported by her social environment, basic faculties and capacities for developing trust and intimacy were poorly developed in

Lauren. The memories of her abuses thus remained secret, only to surface with symptoms ranging, at first, from mild depression to later suicide attempts. In effect, social denunciation had deadened any outward expression or inner reflection.

Many of my clients exhibit a marked reluctance to initiate their account. Particularly they fear reliving the events or demonstrating a predictable emotional reaction. They do not want to risk having their sexual exploitations trivialized in any way; they are simply too important to them. Despite the message in self-help literature to the contrary, many do not want to be told that their responses or their stories are typical. They, moreover, frequently express a fear that their language will be inadequate to describe their experience and thereby render it trite. Another related concern is that the actual expression of an event might result in some distortion, because 'once words have been framed the thought is changed and limited by the very words selected' (Douglas 1966, 64). For these reasons, there are serious risks for the client in expressing something that is deeply intimate and important.

Lauren's therapeutic account explores the intricacies and dynamics underlying the process of narration more effectively than any other client I have witnessed. The immense effort that it took for this account to be constructed is reinforced by Denzin: 'Our humanness and our selfness lie in the words we speak and attach to ourselves. These words, hollow, often empty, learned from others, spoken and written by us, are all that we have' (1989, 78).

When at last Lauren spoke, her first memories of abuse were of childhood incest, violations committed by an older brother. Other incidents of sexual abuse had then followed. She had consistently observed these isolated moments of sexual assault in a disassociated state. She frequently wrote to me that she had watched herself being victimized, 'just the same as if you were watching me. I wasn't in my body.' In Reno's terms, Lauren had to see it 'double' in order to bear what was being done to her (1990, 87).

Lauren was uncertain about the exact onset of her incest, yet she was sure that it had begun prior to the age of five and had ended just before she turned ten. Beyond this, the details remained fragmentary and murky. In fact, as she entered therapy at seventeen years of age, much of her past abuse remained an enigma. She frequently felt depressed and sometimes suicidal. She lived with a gnawing feeling that something was wrong but did not quite understand what it was. She had so suppressed her violations that she did not understand that they could be the root of her depression and self-hatred.

The course of Lauren's narration was not sensational in its style. It contained few dramatic revelations or magnified moments – at least few were communicated. It revealed an extremely slow and self-conscious transformation that began and was sustained in a state of silence. It emerged through therapeutic exchange and an evolving vision of past events through 'guarded, disclosive communication' (Goffman 1959, 192), first in the form of silence, then through writing, and finally in spoken communication.

From the onset of therapy, Lauren expressed discomfort with any abstractions of her experience, and she remained uneasy with most forms of analysis. She evaded psychoanalytic labels and related attempts to brand her experience. She wanted simply to exorcize her story in hope of finding relief from physical and emotional suffering. Yet as she tried to speak of her abuses, she found the procedure too painful. Again, her continuing silence spoke loudly, and it would later say much about account formation. In some significant ways, this silence was as revealing as any narrative could have been.

From her initial incapacity to communicate her account, I assembled a great deal by way of insights and information regarding Lauren's experience. For instance, it informed us broadly about what therapeutic projects of narration elicit on the social positioning of victims of sexual violation. In this regard, Lauren seemed to already know what Maurizio Catani had discerned: 'Speaking of oneself and integrating oneself into a continuity are two ideologically contradictory trends in our civilization' (1981, 214). Exploitation narratives reflect such a contradiction. On the one hand, narrators want to reintroduce wholeness and continuity in their lives in the wake of the intrapersonal fragmentation that follows their abuse and recognize that speaking of their trauma might eventually restore this to them. On the other hand, they know that giving expression to their abuse violates a social code. Doing so could thus disrupt their significant relationships and fragment and disturb their stored memories. Combined, these factors represent for some clients a threatening if not entirely prohibitive level of dissonance.

At the beginning of our exchange, Lauren expressed deep reservations and fear about entrusting her account to me. She anticipated that her telling would result in giving more of herself away, a devastating prospect, especially after having had victimizers take so much from her. In the first stages of our work together, Lauren did not therefore allow any emotional opening that might provoke some further violation of her. Later, in presenting her past abuses for the first time, she divulged only the scantiest outline of what had happened. She then remained almost entirely mute about her most private experiences, a state that lasted for months, as she gauged my reactions while we talked around less painful issues.

Lauren had little reason to trust in the therapeutic alliance. Her trust had already been twice violated by other counsellors through breaches of confidentiality. It was crucial, given this history, that therapy not be invasive before she chose it to be. Yet despite her entrenched misgivings about speaking, Lauren returned, without fail, for her weekly appointments. This indicated that she might eventually risk allowing me access to her secrets. In the meantime our silent alliance represented a symbolic interaction. I acted as witness to a silence that symbolized for her the horror, violation, and devastation of trust she had previously endured.

Remaining wordless about her sexual abuse possessed a clear and comprehensive advantage for Lauren. Most importantly, it was her key to controlling terrible feelings. For her, silence further staved off having her harshest judgements of herself verified by a listener. It likewise prevented her from being disbelieved, of being further violated, or of discovering once again that she was quite alone with her nightmare after having made herself vulnerable. It was thus through her silence that Lauren initially defined her terms and place within the therapeutic interaction. This silence kept her very much in control of her account. While waiting for some further verbal expression from Lauren, I acquiesced and honoured her silence about her story as a self-designed safety strategy, recognizing that remaining silent had been a successful method for dealing with her abuse.

Lauren's reluctance to entrust her account to anyone was complicated by intense feelings of humiliation and not wanting to remember. It was further compounded by not understanding what had been done to her. How could she articulate what she could not fully realize? Combined, this formed a perspective that impeded the narration and development of her account. But, as we later determined, the single largest obstacle to providing a voice for her account was a fear of putting those experiences into words and saying them aloud. That development, it seemed to Lauren, would threaten the control that her initial silence provided. She was convinced that coupling her voice with the horrors she thought she had successfully severed through silence would reanimate those unbearable parts of her past. Even so, without more verbal exchange about her abuse, any further therapeutic benefits might elude her. Although there was no doubt that some transformation was occurring, Lauren lacked the benefit of reflection that the therapeutic exchange could offer.

Reflexive exchange offers fuller verification of experience and supports social reintegration. In the view of Karl Tomm, a therapist working from White's narrative tradition, the verifications sought by clients can unfold within a process of 'reflexive questioning' (1987, 167–83). This condition highlights autonomy and nurtures the importance of feedback for generating greater levels of insight in the client. He affirms, 'The organizational relationships between any two levels of meaning – content and speech act, content and episode, relationship and life script, cultural pattern and episode, and so on – are circular or reflexive. The meaning at each level turns back reflexively to influence the other' (169). The spirit of the reflexive interviewing technique is then its 'self-referential' quality. It offers a self-referential method of checks and controls over such substantive content in the client's story as personal integrity and balance.

During the course of this reflexive interchange, the therapist has a significant role to play in shaping what is revealed. Or at least this is what usually happens. Things unfolded differently in Lauren's case. It took eighteen months for her to finally provide a more detailed version of her story. During this time, in order to control her own and my emotional responses to her material, she accepted no analysis of her abuse. As well, she carefully regulated the pace at which that it was revealed. She was not going to lose control of the little ascendancy she felt she had. How her account was told, and the inclusion and/or omission of details were other areas where she declined to relinquish authority.

At the onset of our exchange I was consigned to stifle feelings of professional ineffectualness while waiting on the extremely gradual and reluctant unfolding of this story. Lauren's expressed aim was not in sync with the usual therapeutic goals of integration. She wanted simply to get her story 'out' and 'away from her.' The degree to which her style of narration was guarded represented a challenge in my role as therapist. Taking the part of silent audience involved a leap of faith for me because I did not then have confidence in the mere act of telling, free of reflection, as a reparative function. In this way Lauren first showed me that witnessed narration alone was highly purposeful.

Incongruously, Lauren's unique narrative approach underscored the interaction between teller and audience. It characterized the often subtle and symbolic nature of this exchange. How an individual formulates and distinguishes the description that she communicates of her atrocious experience, and, in turn, how the presence of a listener transforms both the telling and the subsequent interpretation, is well illustrated with this particular client.

Most of my clients, Lauren included, enter therapy believing that in order to recover from their traumatic abuse, they must either obliterate their unhappy memories or be controlled by them. The reflexive narrative approach, as my clients eventually come to understand it, does not allow for either extreme. When Lauren began to realize this, she started to relinquish the control that silence had afforded her, by speaking. Somewhat ironically, she later reinterpreted her own silence as a form of imprisonment that had kept her bound to her abuse. In contrast, the voicing of her experience promised her liberation from shame and self-blame. Then, with the discovery that her secrets were omnipotent only as long as she did not speak of them, Lauren quite quickly reasserted some control over her silence.

Expressing the Unutterable

The inclination to speak and the desire to be understood propelled each of my clients toward therapy. Typically, clients tell me at the outset that they need to get their story out in a way that assumes a social connection. Lauren did not trust in the value of a social connection rooted in revealing her abuses to another. For that reason, Lauren's course of narrative expression began with a silent gauging of me in relation to her. As I've mentioned, she then graduated to cautious written communication, and concluded with openly speaking of her abuse. While Lauren's need to communicate her story was probably as intense for her as for others, her need for control over some aspect of her life proved equally resilient. Commencing to write down the unspeakable for me was thus a compromise. In the early stages, Lauren saw letting her story 'out' as a relinquishment of self-control, not as a necessary reintegration with her past. It did however afford Lauren a vital social connection.

Writing is an attempt to assert control over events. This is something that most of my clients came to realize fairly quickly. As Reno analyses it, 'To write a memory requires one to see it double; to place the memory in the memoir of which one is the author is to begin to control it. It is not necessary to make the memory happy to have exerted such control' (1990, 88). Lauren did not initially consider it this way, however. Control had been embodied in silence, not in expression. She tentatively began her written account as follows.

I wrote all of this because I really want to get it out and off my mind. This is bits of everything I can remember. I'm pretty sure this is the order which it happened. I tried to remember how old I was but I get all confused because I couldn't remember. I want to say all of this to get it out ... I'm sorry but I'm having a hard time writing it let alone saying it. But I will do the best I can.

For Lauren the project of voicing her abuse worked contrary to her sense of safety. The prospect of attaining control by embracing and articulating her own fragmentation initially thus represented an impasse for her. In this respect she resembled all of my clients. In the early stages of articulation, the unifying of disparate and unintegrated memories that externalizing the story promises seems a long way off from those first provisional utterances.

My clients' sense of discord is eased, as much as it can be, through the appropriation and integration of symbols into what becomes a general reconstruction of self. Ultimately, this approach may provide the client with an infusion of meaning, wholeness, and universality in her imme-diate world. Most often the desire for the self-understanding it offers prevails over fears of chaos and social rejection. Likewise, when Lauren presented dreams that revealed previously unutterable aspects of her abuse they were one channel through which to voice the inexpressible or unmentionable. They contained a certain sense of unreality for her and consequently distanced her from a direct association between them and her own experiences of sexual violation and incest. In effect, dreams helped Lauren to tell her story without her becoming once again completely consumed by negative feelings and self-judgement.

Because, in Lauren' view, her dreams sprang from a dimension that was disconnected from her waking reality (Sanford 1978), she sup-posed that their content could be expressed without her being held responsible for them. More than anything, this perspective spoke of her sense of guilt about having been sexually exploited. Essentially, Lauren allowed her dreams to initiate the telling of the parts of her story that she was initially ashamed to express. In her view, they abstracted those horrible events. For awhile, these images and metaphors clearly revealed the validity of her own experience while providing Lauren some margin of safety from what, in her view, was my potentially judgemental gaze. For instance, upon delivering up fragments of her story for our mutual examination, Lauren would sit back and wait for me to confirm some self-concept shrouded in guilt and compliance – an emotional product of her repeated childhood victimization (Burgess et al. 1985, 135). In this sense, she was not prepared to take full ownership of the content of these symbols. Nevertheless they were her inner creation and thus represented her reality.

The initial disclosure of her abuse, in the form of memories recovered partially through dreams, was a buffer. Our exploring these symbols together provided Lauren with a way to assess, from behind a thin veil of representations, my belief in her worth and validity. Dreams additionally provided crucial details for the shaping of her account. They helped to fill in the blanks. The dream symbol represented what was too remote and/or difficult to otherwise envisage.

According to James Carey, the general approach that Lauren employed was not altogether uncommon. Such private productions are, in varying forms and for diverse purposes, indeed common to everyone: 'This particular miracle we perform daily and hourly – the miracle of producing reality and then living within and under the fact of our own productions – rests on a particular quality of symbols: their ability to be both representations "of" and "for" reality' (1989, 29). When we become aware of our capacity for production in this particular sense, we are sometimes able to exchange, if only for a brief moment of insight, our own constructions in place of the dominant ones that often speak for us.

For Lauren, not wanting her memories to be real was combined with her accompanying sense of shame that was, in turn, exacerbated by wanting to tell her story. This made these memories problematic. In addition, her lack of conviction about the believability of her narrative influenced what she told and what she retained. Consequently, like that of other childhood sexual-abuse victims, Lauren's memory for details of her traumas, such as its frequency and her age at its onset, was left sketchy in places. Her lack of certainty further contributed to her blatant minimization and partial dismissal of her abuse.

The process of expression was also made more complicated for Lauren by her lack of association with her own words. Denzin writes, 'To live their lives into the words that they speak is what all speakers are after' (1989, 78). This aim is perhaps more vital and yet more remote to one who has been sexually exploited. Because client memories are frequently fragmented and uncertain, they have little connection to her words. Sometimes her stories' moments seem unreal, while at other times they are intensely focused. And when memories, words, and experiences are not integrated, the teller's level of belief in her account is often minimized.

Our therapeutic work on facilitating Lauren's trust in her own memories ultimately provided her with a more reliable time frame for her story. For example, our close review of early childhood photographs, together with Lauren's written and sketched reconstruction of her abuse experiences, somewhat reconciled this fragmentation by helping her to recognize her size, age, and even the colour of the clothes that she was wearing during various incidents of abuse. The desired effect of this effort, and the one that we eventually achieved, is well expressed by Herman: 'Out of the fragmented components of frozen imagery and sensation, patient and therapist slowly reassemble an organized, detailed, verbal account, oriented in time and historical context' (1992, 177). Having thus grounded her experiences in this way, Lauren felt less overwhelmed by chaotic and disconnected sensations and more in charge of areas of her past that had previously controlled her.

Since Lauren's articulations were initially sparse and tenuous, it was important that the subtle allusions of her words and metaphors not go astray. Each of her carefully extracted words had numerous potential inferences. Thus, more than any other client who had preceded her in my practice, Lauren taught me to focus on the immediacy of our exchanges. Her form of storytelling, even in her silence, was truly a symbolic interaction. We thus scrutinized the dimensions of her past that she chose to reveal, the importance that she attributed to each episode of her abuse, and ultimately, the mode of constructing, organizing, withholding, and relaying her final therapeutic account.

Forging a Social Reconnection

My own involvement with Lauren's therapeutic account-formation taught me a great deal about how she and others come to define themselves through their crisis. That Lauren decided to resort to narration rather than remain silent should not by now surprise the reader. Plummer cites just one of the benefits of this process. 'Stories function to gloss over disorder. Indeed, the greater the sensed disorder, the stronger may be the need for stories to create tighter classification, stronger boundaries, rules for living' (1995, 177). Lauren did eventually create a clearer self-definition by means of her account construction, through her relationship with me, her reflective listener, and through an integration of her own material. In the pages that follow, I relay some of her narrative as it was first presented to me in written form.

Lauren began her account this way:

> It all started when I was real young. My older brother sexually abused me.
> I would be upstairs doing whatever when he would call out to me. I
> would listen to him and go downstairs to see what he wanted. When I
> would get down there, he would lock the door in case someone would
> come down, I guess. For the longest time I wouldn't know what was
> wrong. I can remember saying no and crying. He would hurt me. He
> would start touching me and I hated it. He went up my shirt and down my
> pants (jeans). He would keep that up and keep it up; how many times did
> I say no, it hurts. I'd be told to shut up and it would continue. I can remem-
> ber him forcing my head between his legs. I didn't know what to do. I
> would be so scared. This went on for so long.

This first instalment in Lauren's narrative emphasized her repeated
explicit and implied objections to her brother's assaults, which, in turn,
reveal her tendency to self-blame. She had carried a sense of guilt and
responsibility since the onset of her brother's abuse. This censorious
view of herself, as is the case with many clients, grew to form a condition of self-stigmatization in which she remained silent in the hopes of
concealing from others her own sense of degradation.

Goffman observed that concealing negative experiences has a significant influence on our failure to develop trusting relationships. This
operates in two ways. Intimate relationships can be extremely threatening for the person attempting to conceal dimensions of her life, and
those withholding secrets are viewed as undesirable friends.

> Control of identity information has a special bearing on relationships.
> Relationships can necessitate time spent together, and the more time the
> individual spends with another the more chance the other will acquire dis-
> crediting information about him. Further ... every relationship obliges the
> related persons to exchange an appropriate amount of intimate facts about
> self, as evidence of trust and mutual commitment ... Newly formed or
> 'post-stigma' relationships are very likely to carry the discreditable person
> past the point where he feels it has been honorable of him to withhold the
> facts. (Goffman 1963, 86)

In Lauren's situation, this concealment perpetuated her isolation. The
feeling of disgrace that she carried stemming from her undisclosed sexual violations was thus complicated by a sense of social inadequacy
and remoteness.

Prior to developing the trust and approval that she found in our relationship, Lauren had not risked revealing her abuse in any other. Our significant therapeutic association allowed Lauren to foster bonds of trust that were needed but that had not been previously established. The absolution and acceptance she craved took the shape of my uncritically witnessing her nightmarish recollections in whatever form they took, without becoming shocked or tainted by their content and, most importantly, without withdrawing my support for her. Her silence and subtle prompts were Lauren's methods of seeking continual reassurance from me that I knew her violations had not been invited. This was the reassurance she needed most.

Giddens provides a partial rationale for Lauren's social detachment. 'Trust established between an infant and its caretakers provides an "inoculation" which screens off potential threats and dangers that even the most mundane activities of day-to-day life contain. Trust in this sense is basic to a "protective cocoon" which stands guard over the self in its dealings with everyday reality' (1991, 3). But Lauren had never received such an inoculation and had never experienced the insulation of a cocoon. The two sides of self, the personal and the social, were remote to her as a result of her abuse and the social environment that permitted it. Until she fostered a trusting exchange with another person, as she did first in therapy, this inner source of reference linking the two worlds eluded her.

After she had developed a trusting relationship, the establishment of personal authority became the necessary next step towards Lauren's reconstitution of self. Without having taken it, she would have remained wholly dependent upon an external authority for approval and insight. Our therapeutic relationship self-consciously fostered a trusting interchange that encouraged the independent development of Lauren's capacity for self-trust and her construction of a reliable inner authority. This allowed her to ultimately assimilate her fractured self and to reach for new connections and perspectives based on her locally cultivated insights.

Carol Gilligan records a similar progression towards integration in her case study of Sarah, a young woman facing her second abortion and who, like Lauren, was quite estranged from her body. In the excerpt below, Sarah's newly discovered voice is intertwined with Gilligan's:

Reiterating with more confidence and clarity her discovery of an inner voice, she says that her decisions previously 'were based elsewhere, I'm not really sure where, but it was coming from somewhere else.' In contrast, now she feels 'really connected with my insides, really good. I just feel strong in a way I'm not aware of having felt, really in control of my life, not just sort of randomly drifting along.' (1982, 122; Sarah's words in quotation marks)

Despite having a sense of reintegration similar to Sarah's, and a first-ever sense of control, Lauren's recovery, like those of my other clients, was riddled with setbacks. She at times felt strong enough to confront closed-off memories only to be confronted shortly thereafter by more unassimilated content. At one point, for example, she became emotionally immobilized by the memory that she had been sexually violated by several perpetrators at various times. Lauren seemed apparently unable to transcend her belief that, as the assailants had said to her, she was responsible for bringing the abuse upon herself. Sexual-abuse theories on the tendency to repeated victimization of those who have been violated once did little to ease Lauren's sense of guilt (Haugaard and Reppucci 1989, 240).

It was only upon reading a similar account by another who had been sexually abused that Lauren, for the first time, understood what had happened to her and openly contemplated whether she was responsible for her own abuse. Her recognition of a common experience granted Lauren the necessary level of insight and liberation from guilt to move forward with her attempt at psychic synthesis.

I started to read the book you wanted me to read ... It was so true. I couldn't believe things really until I read someone else's story. Some of the feelings were so much like mine. When one of the girls was abused by her older brother she didn't think anyone would believe her, she didn't realize it was wrong. She knew something wasn't right. She felt life wasn't worth living. All of these things I have felt ... as I was reading a couple of things came to me. When [my brother] would make me put his penis in my mouth, he would ejaculate. I never knew what it was until recently. I knew it was something, but I didn't know what to tell you. When I was reading the book, one girl said how he ejaculated in her mouth, and how she got sick to her stomach. I got sick to the stomach, when I read that, and, so I guess that's what it was. The same thing when I had to take it in my hands, all this gross stuff would be on my hands. Then he would put it on my stomach. I feel so stupid that I didn't know what it was he was doing. I hate him so much ... remember when I told you that I thought he made me have intercourse with him. Well, the other night, I woke up, I guess I was dreaming. I had a really bad pain going up through me, I was really hurting. I didn't know what it was ... there was something in the book about physical problems and one of them were unexplained vaginal pain. It's like when reading this book, I don't feel so alone ... I know you are there for me, but it's like someone else besides me is telling parts of my story.

The sense of validation and human connection that Lauren felt in finding an authenticated story was heightened by its practical purpose of supplying information about what had been done to her. Someone else's description offered her words and details that Lauren could not locate. Her social environment had not provided her with a trust-based immunization, and it had failed to provide her with terms for understanding her abuse.

Because Lauren did not have a language to describe her incest, her silence was exacerbated, and her alienation, as a result of not understanding what had been done to her body, was intensified. Additionally, it rendered her prone to accepting textually mediated interpretations of her experience and less well equipped to look inwards for interpretative skills. Elana Newman provides an insight into the roots of Lauren's difficulties:

> Some developmentalists believe that linguistic representation of events among children primarily forms through social interaction. If language is learned and practiced in relation to others, it is quite probable that children will not have the linguistic discriminatory skill to describe or communicate external and internal situations in which they are not trained by parents. (2004, 25)

Lauren's lack of social preparation for describing her violations meant that this role fell upon the therapeutic exchange to fulfil. She was not unlike other clients in that sense. In fact, this focus on restoring language is another example of how our therapeutic work monitors and mediates deficits in symbolic interactions, and represents another reason why the therapeutic environment is an important site for sociological investigation.

Significantly, having read the account of another's experience of exploitation, for the first time Lauren also spoke frankly about her own suicidal thoughts. That too was an issue previously cloaked in disgrace and silence. But because this account of abuse, which we both read, embodied many of the atrocities she was now struggling to admit, Lauren guessed that I could hear her innermost thoughts and the harshest details of her abuse without rejecting or blaming her. Together they freed her subsequent telling. Her description reveals the contradictory sensation of at once feeling liberated by the telling of her secrets and of being simultaneously overwhelmed by the consequential release of even more disturbing material.

> It seems like when I begun to feel better something else will come up. [Another memory surfaced.] It's embarrassing to say but I can remember being downstairs and I had on my pink jogging pants. I ran out of [my brother's] room and there was blood on my underwear. I can remember throwing them in the garbage. I'm so mad because I can't remember what he did to get it there and I don't know. When I think about it I don't think I would want to remember how that got there because I know I will be upset if ... I don't know ... I thought I was doing so good and I was so strong.

In writing this letter to me, Lauren sought reassurance and validation for integrating her growing awareness that her brother had raped her. The external catalysts that had generated Lauren's freedom to divulge this guarded content had been the development of a trusted ally who supported her voice and some restoration of order through an externalization of memories. Memories, however, are typically complex constructions. Like many who endured sexual abuse at a young age, this entry confirms that certain memories of Lauren's abuse stood out for her in a crystalline form against a foggy backdrop. She remembers clearly the colour of her pants, for example, but cannot recall the more vital details of the assault. This and other memories were interspersed with time lapses and memory blocks (Haugaard and Reppucci 1989). Such ambiguity was a concern for her.

Agnes Hankiss remarks on how, even under ordinary conditions, we react to particular life events by according them great symbolic importance and fitting them into presentable form. She writes,

> Human memory selects, emphasizes, rearranges and gives new colour to everything that happened in reality; and, more important, it endows certain fundamental episodes with a symbolic meaning, often to the point of turning them almost into myths ... This mythological rearranging plays a specific instrumental role within the self-regulatory system of the psyche

which allows the subject to smoothly incorporate his past and his own life history into the strategy, or 'script,' of his present life. (1981, 203–4)

What does this observation say about life's non-ordinary conditions? This tendency to selection and rearrangement is heightened by trauma. The exploited person more typically reacts against the randomness to which Hankiss refers, with a remarkable 'rage for order' (Stevens 1982, 130), and through a demand for authenticity and accountability from those sometimes scrambled and sometimes absent memories. The lack of reliability represents almost unbearable fissures in the script and, for many, a perceived loss of control.

The client's restoration of control dominates her agenda in the earliest stage of therapy. As Lauren succeeded in finding more ways to alleviate the self-blame associated with her abuse, which subsequently restored to her some sense of control, her signature appeared on her weekly narrative submissions to me. The first emergence of her signature struck me as symbolizing Lauren's having achieved some integration of her story. Simultaneously, she also began voicing her account. The addition of her voice signalled a turning point in therapy. For one thing, as Elaine Scarry notes, 'The voice becomes a final source of self-expression; so long as one is speaking, the self extends out beyond the boundaries of the body, occupies a space much larger than the body' (1985, 33). Lauren's sense of herself was becoming better defined, and as her confidence grew, she was comfortable occupying more space.

Henceforth, with each success she experienced in exposing dimensions of her account, Lauren was able to venture deeper into her personal reservoir of violations and to express more freely the images drawn from it. Lauren became increasingly open to telling these details of her narrative as she began to perceive that this channel was endorsing her evolution. In a lengthy and crucial confessional letter, Lauren demarcated the incidents that made up her history of abuse. It was this disclosure that led Lauren to add her voice to her account:

I'm writing this so it won't be so hard to say when I have to. I was abused by more than one person when I was young. I will tell it as clearly as I can. Even to write it it's hard because I find it extremely embarrassing. It started with my brother. I would be called downstairs and sometimes I think I would be down there watching t.v. and [he] would make me go in his room. I would be lying there and he would take off my pants and shirt and start touching me. He would lick my stomach. He would have his hands all over my chest. I would be lying there looking up at the ceiling; I'm not sure what was going through my mind, but I felt like it wasn't right ... While I'm looking back at it, it's like I'm outside looking at it all, like you would be looking at me now. This occurred over and over. Another time which sticks in my mind is when I was down there and he would spread my legs apart and put his finger there and his tongue there. I was trying to pull my legs together and he would push them apart. He asked me if I liked it. He asked if it tickled. I can remember crying because he hurt me when he put his fingers there. He said it would be O.K. I felt like I was so afraid. He would lie on top of me with nothing on. He told me he loved me. I have no idea where mom was. He would make me put his penis in my mouth. I can remember mom coming down that time and he put his hand over my mouth. I'm having trouble remembering how I was feeling at that age.

When I would be outdoors playing, there was an older guy next door who would also come out and play. He would always come with me in the tall grass. He would kiss me and put his tongue in my mouth. He would lie on top of me and lick my chest. He would put my hand on his penis. This happened a nice [sic] few times while we played. Someone must have saw it because mom called me home and when I went home there was a police car in the driveway. When I got inside, mom hauled down my pants and slapped me across the backside. I was so afraid when I saw the cops inside ... I never told you this because I find it embarrassing. I find it so hard to believe that I was abused by so many different people. Well, while we were outside, there was another guy [name] and another guy. They made me suck on that guy's penis. Why did I keep going back? Why didn't I stay away from it? Marie sometimes I look at it and I'm the one who looks bad. I'm the one who kept going back for more. Oh my.

I'm not sure when this happened – whether it was before all of this or after – but my Pop [grandfather] also sexually abused me. I can only remember once or twice. I would help him bring in the wood, and when I would come back for more wood, he would haul the door to a little and put his hand down my pants and feel around. I really felt gross, uncomfortable.

Overall, Lauren's narration strengthened her. She began to speak with more authority. Yet, as her letter illustrates at length, Lauren was still unable at this point to express much emotional reaction to these parts of her history. The full integration of sadness, grief, and anger could not be achieved until Lauren felt safe from further physical danger. Her grandfather, who shared a house with her and her abusive brother who returned home occasionally, represented valid and enduring threats.

With the death of her grandfather and the long-term imprisonment of her AIDS-afflicted brother, this peril finally subsided. She was, then, for the first time in her memory, free from living with the ceaseless threat of sexual danger. This change also fostered a palpable freeing of her verbal and emotional expression, thus making the earlier episodes of abuse less difficult to communicate. Lauren called me on New Year's Day to relay the news of her grandfather's death. Interestingly, her reaction to the death was not in line with how she believed she *should* respond. Lauren admitted that she could barely hold herself back from celebrating but felt that this was not an appropriate reaction. Once again she sought validation for her feelings. She conceded that her grandfather's suffering in the final weeks of his life represented a form of justice for her. She said, 'He made me suffer for all those years, now it's his turn.' That her grandfather died on New Year's Day was a symbol not lost on Lauren. This serendipity spoke of a new beginning and punctuated her yearning to celebrate while other family members mourned. En route to her grandfather's funeral, Lauren felt elated when she, as she in her own words expressed, 'saw the shed where it happened and knew it wouldn't happen to me again.' Of the burial itself, Lauren said, 'While everyone else was crying and sad, when they threw the dirt on the casket I felt free.'

This death and her emotional reaction to it helped prepare Lauren for the reaction she would undergo after learning of her abusive brother's terminal illness and imprisonment. Directly upon receiving that news, Lauren articulated a sense of relief and underwent an outpouring of still-buried memories of his incest. Once again, a harmonizing of internal contradictions proved crucial for the promotion of unity as she simultaneously sifted through toxic recollections and embraced overwhelming relief.

Before this time Lauren had never had a freely uttered, anecdotal involvement with her memories. The deaths of her brother and grandfather helped Lauren to reconnect to memories that had been rendered alien, first by others' denial of them and then by her negation of them. And through therapy, Lauren learned to give credence to her subjective experiences and locate the self-authority to express submerged and denied dimensions of her abuse. She was then able to cease agonizing over and doubting each memory and could begin to respect them as a source of her own validity. Equally importantly, she no longer dreaded what might emerge.

Myerhoff articulates well the value of that interconnectedness Lauren had restored to herself. 'There is perhaps an area where reflexivity and self-centeredness touch, possibly the point from which they both originated: the restoration of subjectivity as a serious attitude, a basis for gaining knowledge and evaluating it, a ground for making decisions and taking action' (1992, 313). Yet in order to reach this level of respect for her subjective processes, Lauren first required social validation. Because her violations were originally negated at the social level, this is where acceptance optimally needed to occur. Therapy provided for Lauren that necessary intermediary between the private and social world. Her subjective world remained a hostile, foreign entity to her until that point in therapy when language was located. It was only when her abuse account was communicated that her self-construction could be reflected back to her.

The instances of abuse told here, mostly in Lauren's words, sketch the formerly secret horror that she once believed to be insurmountable. Throughout our contact Lauren gave very little consideration, beyond a passing mention, to the fact that prior to entering therapy she had no person in her life who would hear of, let alone confirm, her severe victimization. This isolation was exacerbated still more by her having been punished by her mother for 'allowing' herself to be so victimized. Because she had only ever known isolation, this event had not been especially significant to Lauren. Yet from a social and therapeutic vantage point, it was decidedly noteworthy. Only later did she come to appreciate the intrapersonal and social complications that had arisen because she had never been believed. Companionship through her reconstructive process allowed Lauren to voice her experiences so that she too, through reflection, could see them as valid.

While the experience of therapy provided Lauren with a means of reflecting back upon herself, thereby enabling her to take a second look (Myerhoff 1992), for years she had been avoiding this potentially terrifying process. The reality of therapy became a very different experience from what she had anticipated. In the protected counselling environment she could assemble and amend her account until it sounded and felt like her own, as opposed to a distant nightmare. The reflexive work of redefining herself allowed Lauren to consciously integrate her history of abuse and to distinguish herself in terms of it. Eventually, she shed much of the residual shame that she had carried with her surrounding her forced sexual submission. Lauren's therapeutic narrative production concluded with an easy exchange having developed between us. It followed the course of what had been an excruciatingly slow account construction that sometimes, as a result, had been agonizing to listen to. Ultimately, Lauren was able to externalize the secrets that had overpowered her in her silence. It was this act of making her private account public that effected the reflexive reconstruction. It broke her state of social isolation and literally reconnected her most powerful social tool – her own voice.

Watching Lauren's slow progression towards a vocalization of her plight, and the subsequent emergence of her newly formed self, made me aware of generally how important it is to read women's marginality from the context of a particular reality. My specific analysis of Lauren, for instance, crystallizes a lack of unification with the social, transferred to the level of the self, and stresses a need for sociological intervention in the form of research. Plummer observes, 'One of the central strategies of infusing life is to tell a life: many problems require a strong personal story to become well established. The public domain cannot take too much abstraction: it needs a "life" to make the elements of the story cohere into a public issue' (1995, 129). Lauren's story, and indeed those of all my clients, represents this contention.

The central and particular issue of silence in the above account, as I have discussed, casts light on the generalized social complexities of identity construction following sexual exploitation. Lauren's silence thus reflects a wider social issue, one that such personal experiences provide vast insight into. In her probing of women's voice, Gilligan observed something of what Lauren first demonstrated and then came to know: 'People do not lose their voices; they lose the desire or the courage or the will or the ability to use their voices to tell their stories ... they have taken on the voice of another as their own ... a voice is seemingly lost or confused with another voice that finds more cultural resonance and thus carries more authority' (1982, 173). Because of her intense socially promoted disbelief in herself, and the tenuous nature of her narration, Lauren's account illuminates this point better than most. The magnitude of her own perceived social difference and her testimonial to the rejection she endured was subtly discernible in her silence. As silences like Lauren's are given more serious attention in social research, it is hoped that the patriarchal social construction of denial that has helped to foster them will be diminished.

At the conclusion of therapy, Lauren was able to refer to episodes of her story that, because of its negation by others and in combination with her own sense of degradation, had been, for her, literally unspeakable. Her silence was a metaphor that said so much. But it was her eventual capacity to express and integrate her narrative that had tremendous personal significance. This is the result that she had originally sought in therapy.

5 Private Worlds, Public Worlds, and the Pursuit of Certainty

The previous chapter addressed the complex and often subtle process of a client's externalizing her account. This chapter is concerned primarily with a subsequent phase – the relationship between a narrator's self-perception and the story's public reception. In therapy, this represents the juncture when the client's intrapersonal self begins to scrutinize her public persona in order to locate a synthesis and reconciliation of the two selves, without sacrificing one to the other. How these intrapersonal and public elements interact to shape the narrative is, in part, what produces not only the unique quality of each story's telling but also its therapeutic complexity.

My clients have a personal and social urge to narrate. But when their tentative, sometimes fragmented, and frequently concealed experiences of abuse are compared to external standards of validity, internal discord often results. Their emergent certainties in such instances do not match the objectified social meaning attached to their experience. In order to stay loyal to their own legitimate representations of reality, clients eventually feel compelled to reject external standards in favour of their own. Accommodating this inner unification requires a great leap of faith in themselves and others because, in so doing, they come face-to-face with the possibility of further social isolation.

For those already marginalized, this therapeutically facilitated leap of faith holds benefits. Through the reflexive process described earlier, the client makes innovative and autonomous decisions that allow her to integrate her trauma(s) and reconstruct what is for her a more productive relationship with them and her social world. How she organizes and expresses her account, in conjunction with the therapeutic analysis that develops in its unfolding, brings the teller closer to a personal construction of her reality that is more authentic. This combination of reflection and analysis instils in the client a form of certainty, both in relation to herself and others.

Years of facilitating clients' exploitation narratives has demonstrated what Lauren's story particularly confirmed, that a solitary analysis of their multiple abuses with the therapist is not sufficient for fostering reintegration. Nor in and of themselves do clients' accounts quell the pervasive anxiety that flows from the chaos and randomness in their lives. Their accounts must also reflect and integrate the clients' responses to dominant cultural interpretations of their sexual exploitations. Whether their reactions to these external influences are positive or negative is not at issue here. What is essential is how clients become conscious of and integrate these significant exterior perspectives. As Elana Newman suggests, 'Disentangling the cultural messages from the experienced events can allow a survivor to create self-empowering meaning' (2004, 30).

Our self-referential experiences, according to G.H. Mead, are known to us largely through social conventions and their variations, such as language (Maines 1993, 10). This is where we discover our notions of 'truth' and validity. When my clients' experiences of exploitation do not coincide with broader social objectifications of their experiences, they become isolated and tend to question their own 'truths.' The therapeutic role in these instances is to act as a conduit and mediator between public and private 'truths' in a dialogic or reflexive manner. The therapist interprets public discourse with the client so that she may then locate where there is common meaning and where there is not. It is the sociologist's role in this context to help explain the client's meaning, or subjective 'truth,' to those who want to understand it and add it to the broader discourse.

In this chapter I explore Annie's story, the last and the shortest of the narratives included in this study. Her narrative is distinctive among the sexual violation accounts I have witnessed because the memories of her abuse were so few and splintered. Yet the negative effects of what she recalled, and similarly what she could not recall, proved profound. Furthermore, Annie's private struggle with memory highlights a wider public concern with the believability of sexual-abuse narratives (Cornell 1995), one often shared by the clients themselves. This apprehension is prevalent in Annie's fragmented narrative, through which she recurrently questioned the validity of her own memory. The value and legitimacy of this fragmented memory finally came to light in our quest to locate and integrate narrative content, and was clearly instructive. The manner in which Annie's insights and sense of self surfaced through dream fragments, and the way in which they were pieced together over the course of years of therapy, reflect how lived but nearly forgotten experiences can artlessly surface from the past and help to create personal continuity (see Kohli 1981, 65).

Private Doubts, Public Doubt

Very early on in my practice I wanted all of the pieces of each account to fit neatly together, like a jigsaw puzzle. I thought only then would the status of what were to me questionable details and inconsistencies in my clients' stories of abuse become validated. Even though I acutely wanted to trust my clients' perceptions of their experiences, some of the stories' details, for example, seemed at times simply too severe to accept at face value. In fact, clients' accounts of their abuse were, occasionally, so horrific, as to be almost inconceivable to me. The traumas that they relayed often seemed too many and too unrelenting to have happened to any one individual alone. Moreover, some narratives appeared to be so casually conveyed and devoid of emotion that they did not seem real. Needless to say, I now hold another view.

Despite my initial doubts, I summarily realized that I could not impress my standards of validity upon my clients without escalating the risk of cutting them off from their own tenuous sense of reality. Therapeutically and ethically, such an imposition struck me as a violation of a client's developing sense of self. With more clinical experience, my initial impulse to mend and control their stories was transformed. I came to know instead that listening carefully to these stories, as Paul Thompson has said, 'make[s] us confront the violence that can be done to other peoples' consciousness by imposing our own terms on it' (1981, 293). This was made particularly evident to me as I observed some of my clients urgently probing their memories to locate some objective 'truth' of their childhood violations in order to 'prove' that they had indeed happened. This pursuit only stifled and delayed their reconstruction.

I found out too that the kinds of proofs that I had been seeking to validate their stories were identical to the types of assurances that my clients sought. Like Annie, they wanted their memories to be seamlessly connected and for them to unfold in a clear chronological sequence (see Kohli 1981). Social acceptance was so crucial to them that they viewed their own stories from the outside looking in, and they tried to adjust them to fit some social measurement of validity. Most clients clung, in varying degrees and duration, to this pursuit of locating some external substantiation of their experience. By forcing their stories to exist within the rigid parameters of someone else's definition of legitimacy, clients focused their energies on exactitudes and proof, an impossible goal, instead of on the wider and more holistic mission of rebuilding a fragmented self.

Furthermore, some clients denied their experiences of abuse, or they disassociated from them, in efforts to surpass their pain. So strong was their reluctance to assimilate their abuse, that, prior to therapy, many had attempted to live as though these violations were not their own. Given their own resolve to reject their abuse, how could they then expect others to accept it? Yet at some level, all of my clients knew what had happened to them, and they wanted others to recognize their experiences as 'truth.' Consequently, the intensity of the social doubt that was cast upon them after telling their accounts to their families, trusted community members, or the justice system was emotionally shattering. Some clients' stories were discounted outright as having been fabricated or as the product of false memories (Vella 1992). Therapeutically, such blatant public scepticism stifles the victim's will to speak and alters the content of her account in order to have it conform to a socially manufactured standard.

The issue of false memory syndrome is an intriguing metaphor for this abiding private and public tension over what constitutes 'truth' and 'reality.' This syndrome is a psychological label whose appeal and authority continues to develop, as it becomes increasingly applied in legal cases and more widely in public discourse, in public efforts to diminish or dismiss recollections of sexual abuse. The general public suspicion and/or wish that memories of childhood sexual abuse have been planted in clients by counsellors, psychotherapists, and the like is vocal and influential. Of course this commanding collective desire to disbelieve also greatly increases the clients' vulnerabilities as they seek to externalize their experiences of exploitation.

In 1995, William F. Cornell wrote a lengthy review of the literature on this volatile subject. In his effort to address the growing controversy over the legitimacy of memories surrounding sexual abuse, he called for 'balance – and a measure of ambiguity' (1995, 4), and argued,

> The risk of creating pseudo-memory in psychotherapy cannot be ignored.
> However, an even greater risk is that a therapist's biases will impose a pre-

mature limiting meaning on the client's emerging affective experiences when they actually reflect a range of disturbing factors, including shock trauma, strain trauma, environmental failures, intrapsychic conflicts, and lost dreams and desires. (10)

Here, Cornell identifies the crux of the matter, certainly as my practice has communicated it to me. Given that a trauma exists, the greatest threat that false memory poses does not reside in the debate between 'truth' and 'untruth' but in the potential imposition of a therapist's version of validity upon a client's story. In overwhelming a client's realities or supplanting those with one's own, the therapist risks eroding the client's self-perception, diminishing her authority, and undermining therapeutic potential.

In order to combat and transcend the corrosive effects of intrapersonal and public disbelief, as well as to guard against the imposition of an alternative validity upon a client's narrative, part of our therapeutic mission is the disentanglement of her version of her abuse accounts from others' perceptions of what they should look or feel like. These professional insights can then be reflected back to her in moments of renewed self-doubt. In order to locate meaning from such insights, we found it necessary to take the spotlight off 'truth' itself and to approach, from a different angle, the issue of legitimacy and worth in the client's narrative. The epistemological antidote that we found, which was indisputably authentic and capable of fostering reconstruction, lay in the process of account construction.

As already discussed, the therapeutic account is usually spontaneously delivered and has potential for transforming the teller's perceptions of past and present events. The process we developed together replaced their unattainable pursuit of verifiable 'truths' and became the new joint focus of our therapeutic deliberations. The insights and transformations, themselves an expected outcrop of the account's creation, often provided enough validity to satisfy most clients. It came to replace that former insistence on external validation. Even when clients could not, in every situation, distinguish unreality from reality, or nail down the exact circumstances out of which their memories sprang, the inherent value of things even partly remembered became obvious to us both. By means of researching their respective exploitations, these clients learned that it was vital to give primary credence to these experiences in whatever form they presented themselves.

'Truth,' that external standard by which these greatly unpleasant and once-secret experiences were evaluated and/or dismissed, ultimately

became a mere byword in our therapeutic dialogue. Individual transformation usually began with the client's acknowledgement that if she
were to be judged exclusively on the basis of external definitions of
validity, then her account might be rendered improbable. This shift
from spotlighting externally rendered forms of validity to a recognition
and acceptance that the reconstruction of identity is of foremost importance, ultimately affected every client's therapeutic experience. It
involved a personal evolution that all who continued to struggle for
self-acceptance eventually adopted.

Annie's Fragmented Memory

In contrast to my other clients, who expended much of their energy
prior to therapy attempting to repress their negative memories, Annie
was remarkable in the intensity of her endeavour to remember exactly
what it was that had happened to her as a child that had left her feeling
so emotionally empty and devastated. Despite years of probing, Annie
had only a scattering of clear memories from the first eleven years of
her life.

Having worked with abused women and children, Annie was well
familiar with the signs and symptoms of sexual abuse. She stated at the
onset of therapy that many of her feelings and behaviours mirrored
those of others who had also been sexually abused (Haugaard and Reppucci 1989). Yet mere recognition of this fact, or the possibility that similar abuses might have occurred to her, did little to advance a
reconnection with her past, because memory loss denied her the access
she sought. She felt that, at best, she had only 'superficial' symptoms
and intangible feelings to work with. Initially, Annie could locate no
method to ease her sense of fragmentation.

Together, we explored old photographs, we experimented with
'active imagination,' and independently she pursued hypnosis – all to
no avail. Only through examination of her dream symbols did Annie
finally begin to rediscover some of her emotional life from childhood,
and eventually she was even able to recall a few relatively distinct memories. To a limited degree this achievement helped her to discern who
she had been and what her environment had been like in those once
entirely unreachable years. The dreams she produced during the course
of therapy, all recalled from earlier times, triggered a string of memories
that helped her reconstruct some sense of her physical and emotional
identity. These gradually recovered dimensions of her experience even-

tually combined to ease her perception of complete barrenness and 'loss' for an eleven-year period of her life.

Sexual-abuse accounts are commonly compared to Swiss cheese because they are full of holes. The principal issues that motivated Annie to seek therapy were indeed directly attributable to those perforations in her life she could not fill in with memory. On the basis of much clinical corroboration, I now view these gaps in memory as entirely consistent with trauma recollection, or of not recalling, as the case may be. This assessment, however, did little to ease Annie's disquiet over trying to exist without portions of her history.

Her desperation to infiltrate her closed-off memories at the onset of therapy brings to mind Clifford Geertz's remark: 'Whatever sense we have of how things stand with someone else's inner life, we gain it through their expressions, not through some magical intrusion into their consciousness. It's all a matter of scratching surfaces' (1983, 373). Geertz's observation was made from the standpoint of the ethnographer and outsider, endeavouring to look into another's experience. His comment imposes boundaries on subjective and objective standpoints as though these realms are completely discrete. Yet Annie felt like an outsider within her own experience. At the onset of therapy, she was desperately scratching the surfaces of her own life, attempting to find more substance with which to fill in some very large blanks.

As a result of the absent memories, and the outsider status that they evoked, Annie was emotionally impassive, with one important exception. Anger was the single response that she presented effortlessly. When she stopped binging on alcohol, her anger subsided, but, as Annie said, 'so too did most feelings.' Anger had been a problem for her, yet she had also known it to be truly her own when she could claim so little else. Communicating other emotions produced in Annie such extreme panic that even anticipating an expression of feeling left her, quite literally, short of breath. To be comfortably reconnected with her feelings was thus one of Annie's primary therapeutic goals. This, however, was a difficult task, in light of the fact that she had so few concrete memories to connect with, for a significant part of her childhood. Consequently, she attempted to reconstruct her account with whatever became available.

Annie's desire to confront mounting problems with alcohol abuse and anger had prodded her to enter therapy. As they were with other clients, these were merely catalysts that forced her to examine myriad underlying emotional and social problems that, we discovered, could be directly traced to earlier sexual victimization (Morrow and Smith 1995). Annie had long carried within her the sense that she had been sexually violated, as a child, in instances other than those her memory permitted her to recall. But for Annie, and for others, a prevalent concern was how she could first uncover and then view as valid her own experience of sexual abuse, even though others might disbelieve her story and possibly even reject it.

Annie's life was exceedingly difficult for her to piece together. It was not only filled with large blank spaces, but it was also peppered with bits of memory, some of which belonged she knew not where (Gagnon 1981). While some memories of people, incidents, and places had returned to her over a span of many years, she could not always find them a proper chronological home. Somewhat of an anomaly among my clients, Annie felt that she could not locate enough material to accurately reconstruct her life, even for herself. This left her intrapersonally alienated and made the telling of her narrative tentative and episodic. As a listener, I found it confusing and difficult to position experiences that lacked the typical reference points and chronological sequence, a reaction that emphasizes our more general cultural reliance upon order in account communication. My own disorientation gave me insight into the sense of chaos Annie sometimes endured in trying to order her memories.

While I was frequently confused about time and place in Annie's unfolding account, the narrow parameters of her memory did not for me call her account into question in the same way as it did for her. These voids did not compel me to invalidate her experience. I recognized, as Denzin has, that narratives can be shifting and inconsistent. 'Stories then, like the lives they tell about, are always open-ended, inconclusive and ambiguous, subject to multiple interpretations. Most slowly unwind and twist back upon themselves as persons seek to find meaning for themselves in the experiences they call their own' (Denzin 1989, 81). Total recollection was not a yardstick that we used to assess the value of narrative within our therapeutic dialogue. And given the often unfixed nature of the narrative form, Annie's fragmented account was quite unexceptional. But the extent of her memory loss was not.

As she gradually relayed her account, Annie became increasingly concerned with its acceptability in the outside world. She viewed it always from a double perspective. From the vantage point of fractured memories and disconnected feelings – all that she had to reconstitute her identity with – it was valid to her: 'It felt right.' However, in screening her process and findings through the critical eye of a detached observer, she believed that they fell consistently short of objective 'truth.' She presumed that this approach to reclaiming content from her past life through dreams, would, by external interpretations of validity, be regarded as suspect if not baseless. Getting Annie to view her experience from inside of her was therefore our biggest challenge. Yet gradually, through the unconscious production of dream metaphors and a burgeoning trust in her conscious work with them, Annie first touched upon and then grew to esteem her subjectively rendered perspective.

The problem of unearthing terrible experiences is multifaceted. A vast measure of each sexual-exploitation account desires to remain unspoken. This reticence is due not only to the teller's self-consciousness about her own believability, but also because the victim, for any one of a multitude of reasons already mentioned, cannot comprehend her own experience. Plummer is also interested in those remote parts of the narrative. He writes, 'I am speaking here about experiences hidden from awareness and part of this means entering the world of the unconscious: of repressions, masks, denials. Much of the inner life is kept at bay, sealed off from any potential for story telling' (1995, 127). Therapy, as I practise it, makes conscious what is concealed so that vital understandings do not remain socially inaccessible. Ultimately, in order for an account to be transformed into something that is personally as well as culturally significant, it needs to be translated from the realm of the unspoken or barely audible to a more widely comprehensible experience. Yet Annie's situation presented an unusual obstacle to achieving this end. We needed to establish equilibrium between actively seeking out those closed-off memories and respecting her need to leave some content unreachable.

Early on in our contact, Annie presented what she called her 'one vivid memory' of childhood sexual violation. 'I am standing in a closet with a man. He exposes his penis to me. I reach my hand out to touch his penis. He yells at me not to touch him. I am aware that my brothers are close by playing – either inside the house or outside nearby the house.' As it turned out, the man in this memory was a friend of Annie's parents. Many years after this incident when Annie was a teenager, he asked her if she remembered going over to his house on Sundays. In order to avoid the confrontation that revealing this memory might well have invoked, Annie told him that she did not. She did, however, remember this fragment acutely and with all her senses, and repeatedly expressed concern about those Sunday visits that she had no memory of.

In addition to this episode, Annie lived with another memory, or rather a 'strong sense,' that her eldest brother had sexually molested her when she was a child. Annie had a recollection of this brother that was particularly disturbing for her, because she felt it to be sexually inappropriate: 'He is trying to take my clothes off to prepare me for bed. I am lying on the top bunk of my bunk beds holding my body rigid so that he cannot pull my tights off.' Annie described a subsequent experience of discomfort around sexuality whenever she was in his presence. She also described feeling an 'intense urge to flee' when returning home, as an adult, after a long absence and catching sight of this brother on the porch of her parent's home. Later Annie presented numerous dreams in which he played the role of a sexual perpetrator.

A third recollection of sexual violation was, in her mid-teens, of being molested by a physician in whose care she had been placed. He was initially 'kind' to Annie. He 'comforted' her and 'listened' to her in what she described as 'a period of great emotional pain and physical illness.' He then came into her hospital room when he was supposed to be off duty, ordered a sedative for her, and, 'smelling of alcohol,' then proceeded to molest her by fondling her breasts and genitals. In our therapeutic exchange Annie confided to me that she had trusted him. By that point in her life, she had received so many hurts and violations that trust was rare, and that violation, she said, in an exceptional moment of vulnerability, 'broke my heart and closed my last door on trust.'

Apart from these recollections, of the many more or less complete dreams that Annie eventually offered for analysis, there was one mere fragment that she returned to again and again. Initially, the dream's message went unheeded as she attempted to expel other recollections from her lost period. But this dream, Annie later decided, spoke directly to the mystery she was attempting to unravel. She recalled, 'Someone before me is holding up a sign that reads, "It was too long ago and too deep."' Viewing this dream as bearing a direct relationship to her search for reintegration, she explained, 'This tells me that my hurt is too great and occurred too long ago for me to recall it.' Toward the conclusion of her therapy, she chose to heed the dream's advice and respect its message.

In general, the dreams that Annie identified in counselling as transitional or pivotal in contributing to a fuller comprehension of her episodic life fell into three broad categories. Each one reiterated issues that

Annie consistently returned to in her account and aided her integration of negative feelings whose origins she could not recollect. One symbolic theme involved pursuit, a second dealt with searching for things that had been lost or stolen, and a third dealt with reconnection to parts of herself that she felt to be missing. From these dreams, Annie extracted a broader understanding of herself. She interpreted the dream metaphors not literally, although literal meanings frequently beckoned, but as containers of insight that held wider and deeper meanings. In these metaphors she read the simultaneously intrapersonal and universal qualities of her experiences. Annie recognized them as embodying the breadth and depth necessary for explicating her intervals of lost memory. She viewed them also as tools that would enable her to recognize and integrate her past as her own and authorize her to reconstruct her identity.

Interpreting and Reconstructing Identity

Annie's abiding mistrust of her own emotional expression was tied to her lost memories and associated hurt from various assaults. She was apprehensive about anything that appeared to threaten her controlled and principally cognitive process of dealing with intruding feelings. On the one hand, this strategy, as previously noted, had not served her entirely well, as it blocked her from pursuing necessary alternative paths. On the other hand, some of her dream images seemed to be so closely aligned with her recollections that, in spite of her will to maintain control, she became emotionally connected with them.

Because the issue of whether or not to pursue her lost memories was an ever-present and unresolved stress, Annie frequently conjectured about whether finally confronting those elusive memories would be as distressing as her unrelenting pursuit of them. She wondered too if her incessant search for memories of sexual violation was 'killing' her, 'consuming' her, or threatening to 'control' her. All three of these potential effects were suggested in the following dreams. In addition to posing these possibilities they aided in restoring an emotional equilibrium to Annie's life. The first dream presents a situation very much akin to Annie's ongoing waking quandary:

> I am trying to save the life of a child from a man who is trying to kill the child. The man chases me. He is driving a bicycle. I am on foot. I know that he will not kill me but he will attempt to own me, control me, or consume

me. There is a sexual overtone to his potential consumption of me. I arrive at the edge of a cliff. Across the abyss in front of me are two very tall trees. These trees have no horizontal branches. If I jump across the abyss and reach the trees I will be safe. I think the trees are birch. I might die if I attempt to leap across the cavern and do not make it.

Annie's most pressing thought upon waking from this dream was essentially a summation of her existing dilemma: 'I am faced with a decision. Should I risk dying for security or stay where I am and face what is pursuing me?'

She also recognized that the dream's birch trees signified strength for her, as they were firmly rooted in the ground. Her immediate general identification with trees was linked to one of Annie's few childhood memories. She recalled a tree-filled cemetery near her home, where she used to go 'to think and hide.' The potential leap toward those trees suggested unpredictable consequences. Annie had no way of knowing whether or not her dream's jump would conclude safely. Since the trees 'had no horizontal branches to grab hold of,' there was not much room for error. In her waking discussion, she calculated that her leap toward the trees had to be on the mark. The life of a child was dependent on her landing safely on the other side, yet she was risking her own life to save that child. In interpreting 'the other side' as perhaps representing a return to those times she could not recall, she wondered if there was any tangible security or insight to be gathered from such a move. Or did the leap to the other side represent a continuation of a fruitless pursuit of certainty? This dream, as well as the many other questions and interpretations that grew out of it, initiated for Annie a new way of thinking and talking about her search.

A later dream continued this theme of being confronted with a difficult decision in the midst of a seemingly dangerous pursuit:

I am travelling on foot with a child. We are looking for 'Him.' We come to a rustic cabin. Its furnishings are basic, simple. The cabin is empty but there is a feeling that someone will be returning if we wait. A wolf approaches the cabin door. I shut the door just in time to lock it out. As I am shutting the door on the wolf I wonder if it actually poses a threat.

In working with this dream, Annie made several discoveries. She identified her search for 'Him' as a quest for acceptance and inner peace. Although she readily recognized the 'Him' of her dream as representing God in the formal sense, it was a secular interpretation of God's essence that she was seeking to restore in her personal life. Here, as in the previous dream, she was travelling with a child in need of protection. Once again, she viewed this child as representing a dimension of herself. According to Annie, the dream's simple cabin and its soon-to-return owner represented, in riddle form, the potential answer to her search. And the wolf signified what had been pursuing her in her waking reality. Like the man in her former dream, the wolf threatened to consume her but was not necessarily dangerous.

Whenever Annie felt disposed towards a return to her linear pursuit of objective evidence, work with such metaphors helped her to refocus the essence of her therapeutic goal: a sense of integration and entrenchment. Her strong desire to supply herself with these qualities redirected us from a fruitless tracking down of vague details and lost memories toward what she had identified as more essential issues. Guided by our reflexive exploration of her dream representation, Annie slowly started acquiring metaphors that affirmed her validity, and she began to value them above her previous search for exterior substantiation. Her images had the additional benefit of developing in her an intuitive approach to understanding her situation.

Another significant dream transformed Annie's perceptions of her search for lost memory in yet a different way. The 'one image or picture' generated in it did not so much raise new questions as it provided her with a stronger sense of self-significance. It located and even grounded her in what she regarded as an intuitive and historical awareness of her own condition of being. She described it this way:

> This dream is really one image or picture. In it I see a line, like an ancestral line, stretching through space. On that line I recognize my grandmother, followed by my mother, followed by me, my daughter, her daughter, and so on in both directions. It is a powerful image for me because it plants me strongly in the midst of a history and a future and alleviates my sense of rootlessness. I have a strong place within this line.

Significantly, this internally rendered metaphor of connectedness was produced and interpreted by Annie and not designed to appeal to another's sense of reality. As with the source of all dream images, this one corresponded with an internal 'reality.' The certainty that it evoked in Annie suggested that an evolution had occurred. Unlike the birch tree of her earlier dream, which was lacking the horizontal branches that may have provided safety in her perilous leap into the unknown, this dream image suggested both upward and outward development. It represented an infinite horizon, of which she was a firm dimension, stretching across the sky. And it was this image that most transformed Annie's perception of herself as one who was fragmented to the point of peril, to one who could be whole.

Annie discovered in this symbolic representation of a society and an entirety the message that the certainties she had been seeking were not external to her. Her sense of balance and belonging, which she was convinced her memory had undermined, was thus intuitively manifested in the image of this shared journey. Accordingly, Annie located the seamlessness of connection that she sought. This symbol was her representation of her own place in history, her present, and her future. Annie thus made a significant connection that grew out of an inner source and proved crucial for formulating an intrapersonal sense of validity. Locating an enhanced sense of interiority made it possible to ground her account.

The Private Narrative's 'Coming Out'

As we noted, Annie was for a time preoccupied with finding proof of her abuse. Her pursuit reflects a wider search for validation. She believed that memories equalled truth and without them her experience was invalid. Her struggle for self-acceptance, likewise, mirrors the objections that many researchers have with studying a subjective form like the narrative. Although, as we have noted, her unconscious and her body offered her other kinds of validation, which she eventually came to acknowledge, they were not traditional forms of empirical proof, and accordingly they are not broadly accepted.

Given the multiple layers of self that become closed off following trauma, internal legitimacy is often difficult for clients to locate or sustain. Nonetheless, for those like Annie who have been sexually violated, the self that symbolically splits away from the body and remains out of reach (Herman 1992) sometimes possesses the remedy for reintegration. Any contradictions between body, mind, and emotions thus need to be resolved in order for clients to distinguish their perceptions as valid. An experience that has been isolated from other dimensions of awareness does not benefit from their full understanding and cannot therefore achieve their authorization.

In seeking some form of reconciliation between the contradictions of their embodied, mental, emotional, and social selves, clients frequently assume a view of themselves that has less to do with self-perception than with social legitimacy. This exterior vantage point was certainly the one with which Annie wrestled most tenaciously. Her concerns about the validity of her perceptions are consistent with those expressed in others' sexual-exploitation accounts. Some of these conflicting versions of self are developed as internal fragmentation caused by the painful secret that the client has carried (Woodman 1990), while others are externally imposed.

Sexual abuse frequently causes such extreme alienation from self and from others that, in its wake, the notion of who one is, or who one is in relation to others, becomes highly disorienting. Through therapy we attempt to reorient the client within these crucial relationships. But the therapeutic relationship is not representative of relationships outside of this sphere. While trust is cultivated here, outside of this environment trust is merely, as Adam Seligman says, 'an ideal model of communal life' (1997, 7). My clients all need to resurface from this sheltered therapeutic setting to test their reconstructed selves on the less than ideal society around them. Initially such public exposure poses a great risk to them, because their newly developed insights are tentative additions to their personal narratives. This raises the question of why the social world holds such a power over the client. I return to this point later.

Sociological arguments and explanations have contributed significantly to our understanding of fundamental questions of self. They have decisively touched matters that intersect with the social components of my clients' reintegration processes. This is material that has prompted the work of illuminating the area between intrapersonal and social understandings of validity. As the therapeutic in turn highlights social dimensions of clients' experiences, and refuses to see them only as intrapersonal constructions, we are freed to explore those voices external to clients that are so influential to their private interpretation of experiences.

G.H. Mead viewed this exchange between the individual and the social or objective world as a cycle of influence. He placed his emphasis on a certain order of evolution, with the social self preceding and allowing the birth of the private and/or subjective self. My concern is with the problematic of the interchange between private and public, as it influences my clients' perception of themselves and the subsequent direction of their narratives. In the following excerpt, Mead captures the underlying dynamic of what subsequently develops for my clients as a self-conscious reflexive plight, as they see their abuse experience from a perspective that is less personal than social:

> It is true that certain contents of experience (particularly kinaesthetic) are accessible only to the given individual organism and not to any others, and that these private or 'subjective,' as opposed to public or 'objective,' contents of experience are usually regarded as being peculiarly and intimately connected with the individual's self, or as being in a special sense self-experiences ... the existence of private or 'subjective' contents of experience does not alter the fact that self-consciousness involves the individual's becoming an object to himself by taking the attitudes of other individuals toward himself within an organized setting of social relationships, and that unless the individual had thus become an object to himself he would not be self-conscious or have a self at all ... in order to become aware of himself ... he must become an object to himself, or enter his own experience as an object. (1934, 225–6)

This dialectic reflects on an issue that intimately concerns my clients. It punctuates a central and ongoing dimension of their reconstructive journey, the relationship between self-construction and social construction.

They as well are inclined to view themselves at some point in an objectified form, as though through another's perception of their experience. They wrestle with this perspective as they attempt to comprehend the language and interpretation of their experience that has been applied to them. In Annie's case, the strength of the external perspective initially propelled her search but also diminished her belief in the validity of her abuse experiences. Yet as we have seen with Annie and other clients, when dealing with the hinterland between subjective and objective worlds, we need to concern ourselves with extremes of over-objectification and the potential loss of self.

In their reflections upon the exchange between public and private that fuels identity formation, Berger and Luckmann support observations that I have also drawn from my practice: 'This is not a one-sided mechanistic process. It entails a dialectic between identification by others and self identification, between objectively assigned and subjectively appropriated identity' (1966, 132). They observe further, and what close co-facilitation of my clients' reconstructions has also revealed, 'We not only live in the same world, we participate in each other's being'

(130). But whereas Berger and Luckmann describe the relationship between the individual and the objective social world as being 'like an ongoing balancing act' (134), I tend to emphasize this process more as the reflexive cycle of transformation I have illustrated throughout.

At the conclusion of therapy Annie had not resolved all concerns about her lost memories. And yet her preoccupation with achieving external validity before her 'certainties' could be called her own was greatly diminished. In short, her private self had reconciled with her public one that, in turn, subdued the external discourse that had previously defined and regulated her self-perception. Through her own metaphors and 'magnified moments' she re-appropriated her identity by reflexive narrative construction. Like most of my other clients, Annie did not have all of the answers. She did, however, locate the process through which to work and she instituted enough inner resolve and discernment of self to restate and renegotiate her public place. As in the metaphor depicting her location in her ancestral line, Annie had established a position where she best harmonized internal and external voices. In this place, Annie found the validity she had sought.

Epilogue: Re/solving the Social Self in Therapy

Sociological work on the self has helped to expound what I have observed and developed in the therapeutic context. For instance, in his discussion of 'what symbolic interactionism is' (1992, 25), Denzin describes the self as 'a multilayered phenomenon' to which he attributes five forms that directly subscribe to our reflexive work with interacting layers of being:

> The *phenomenological self* describes the inner stream of consciousness of the person in the social situation. The *interactional self* refers to the self that is presented and displayed to another in a concrete sequence of action ... self is also a linguistic, emotional, and symbolic process. The *linguistic self* refers to the person filling in the empty personal pronouns (I, me) with personal, biological, and emotional meanings ... The *material self*, or the self as a material object, consists of all the person calls his or hers at a particular moment in time. (1989, 32)

> The material self is also commodified in the exchange relations that the person enters into. The *ideological self* is given in the broader cultural and

historical meanings that surround the definition of the individual in a particular group or social situation. The *self as desire* refers to that mode of self-experience which desires its own fulfillment through the flesh, sexuality, and the bodily presence of the other. (1992, 25)

Some of these features of self, as identified by Denzin, are given a higher profile than others in our analysis. Foremost, this is so because these are the dimensions in which we are working to resolve conflicts. This is also because, as with Annie's fragmentation, my clients are more consciously connected to some dimensions of being than others. Nevertheless all these characteristics have application to how my clients view themselves within their experiences. My own sociological study of sexual exploitation has particularly centred on the ideological self, how that culturally informed and regulated self symbolically interacts with the other roles, and how such interplay comes to light in the therapeutic dialogue.

A multilayered framework of the self is also proposed by Ian Burkitt. He sees the self in terms of dimensions of being that are 'distinct and cannot be reduced to each other, yet at the same time cannot in any way be separated' (1999, 21). One attraction of a perspective that upholds the inseparability of life's dimensions is that it enables us to sidestep altogether the chicken and egg question of whether the private self precedes the public one, or visa versa. The notion that we can never completely locate the point at which one begins and the other ends more closely resembles the perceptions of self that emanate from the depth analysis undertaken with my clients.

Denzin's social research goes a greater distance than others towards elucidating that certain fusion between the intrapersonal and social dynamic that is at once so socially and therapeutically significant. He maintains that one spontaneously overflows into the other in the form of the epiphany. 'The epiphany occurs in those problematic interactional situations where the person confronts and experiences a crisis. A personal trouble often erupts into a public issue, thereby connecting a private trouble with a public response' (1992, 83). My clients' exploitation narratives ground and demonstrate this assertion.

While Denzin acknowledges that epiphanies 'radically alter and shape the meanings which people assign to themselves and their life projects' (1992, 82), he does not explore in any depth how such transcendental awareness is made public, nor how it then reflects back to influence the private interpretation of self. My clients' account formations have inadvertently charted this unique and symbolic space between the personal and public realms. The reflexive structure of their therapy has fostered exchanges between the many dimensions of self and studied, in turn, their relationship to the social. Consequently, rare moments of symbolic interaction have been highlighted through this process.

Another largely unexplored area is the one that exists between the clients' emotional selves and their bodies. Although for many of my clients their disembodiment occurred as a result of their abuse, their first concern is almost inevitably with mending their emotional self and interpreting their emotional fissures through a social lens, or 'ideological' self. The body considered in and of itself as a source of symbolism and communication is arrived at only later. Even then, as I pointed out previously, a self-description based on symbolic embodiment is easier to accept and communicate than a direct expression of what the body has endured, for fear and shame, resulting from many violations, are harboured in the body and are thus associated with it. This repudiation of the body is partly due as well to the inexpressibility of physical pain (Scarry 1985). My present analysis does not linger over my clients' embodied processes though, and this remains a theme for additional research. On the basis of all that I have observed, however, it is evident to me that the emotional self cannot be understood in isolation from the body.

In this regard, sociological literature says much less than therapeutic literature. In calling for 'an adequate understanding of any human phenomenon,' Berger and Luckman merely point out that in their view the relationship between 'organism and self' in a 'socially determined environment' is 'a particularly eccentric one' because 'man experiences himself as an entity that is not identical with his body, but that, on the contrary has that body at its disposal' (1966, 50). Arthur W. Frank states quite candidly that in contemporary sociological theory 'the body remains silent' (1991, 36). And Peter E.S. Freund, whose interest in the social construction of health and illness borders on my own, comments, 'Unresolved tensions in mind-body, society relationships haunt the sociological landscape' (1990, 453). My clients' alienation from the textually mediated language of sexual abuse is not a closed phenomenon. Their gender-related estrangement extends beyond a detachment from this specialized discourse; it warns that, for them, a broader social alienation had occurred. In order to effectively research this fissure within the self, I needed to probe locally and personally in the way that my clients' narratives have done. Yet by also looking beyond their direct experiences to sociology for what is happening, I have unearthed some socio-logical explanations that intersect with and partially explain my clients' experiences. But in this regard, much still remains missing in our under-standing of what private estrangement from the social means in matters of identity construction following sexual abuse.

Among sociologists who have made significant inroads in this direc-tion is Dorothy Smith with her work on women's alienation from pub-lic language. Among other themes, her feminist critique proposes a sociological approach that my clients' lived experiences of therapeutic narration demonstrate. They support Smith's contention that only by a return to the most fundamental aspects of their worlds, which includes their subjective and sometimes unconsciously rendered representa-tions and the language generated for them through these, can they, and ultimately we, make sense of their experience. This necessitates dis-tancing themselves, and ourselves, from 'recipe' knowledge (Berger and Luckman 1966, 66), labelling, or any form of language that gener-ally does not fully touch upon their condition.

My clients also demonstrate the necessity to tell of their abuse through a reinvention of themselves, as the only way of making sense of one's past and one's relation to it. Here, Nikolas Rose's comments are helpful. He urges us to 'invent ourselves differently' (1996, 197). This mission is 'underpinned by the belief that historical investigation can open up our contemporary regime of the self to critical thought, that is to say, to a kind of thought that can work on the limits of what is thinkable, extend those limits, and hence enhance the contestability of what we take to be natural and inevitable about our current ways of relating to ourselves' (2). My clients, through their painful examinations of past sexual exploi-tation, attempt to do just this on a personal level, as they necessarily turn on end their former ways of relating to themselves, and hence to others. In so doing they come to reject most externally rendered definitions of their relationship to themselves, and they each try independently to reinvent themselves. Through therapy, my clients negotiate a place for themselves amidst externally rendered values, judgements, and asser-tions. This work brings them closer to what is personally valid. In addi-tion, the mediation of these other perspectives through the narrative serves a 'restitutive' function, similar in its effect to Hepworth and Turner's notion of confession as a 'ritual of inclusion' (1982, 28). In this way, my clients' private acts of redefinition and reconstruction ease their usual sense of marginalization and reintegrate them into a broader dia-logue, thereby rendering their intrapersonal problems public.

My clients' stories, as told to me in the isolation of my office, always seem to have been intended for a wider but absent audience. This audience of silent witnesses and judges consisted of my clients' abusers, their families, teachers, friends, the larger community, and the experts who have sat invisibly in the background of each telling, and who influenced the nature and character of these accounts by imposing external standards and evaluations upon each woman's private experience of violation. Ironically perhaps, in order for each story to truly become the client's own unique reflection of herself, we have found it necessary to address these external and public voices by including them indirectly in our own deliberations.

Concerns similar to my own about the negative impact of external impositions upon the private account have frequently been echoed in feminist psychoanalytic thought. For example, Shearer-Cremean and Winklemann have centred on the efficacy of women's narratives within a societal discourse that remains patriarchal, thus illustrating the role of patriarchal power in the construction of language:

> In patriarchal discourse women's narratives will always be called into question, doubted, made invisible – even by other women, who may be in denial that the reality of pervasive male violence against them even exists. Thus the female survivor of male violence may never experience the satisfaction of feeling safe or secure. How could she feel safe when her own voice will be always and everywhere vulnerable to uncertainties, shifts, gaps, and collisions of meaning? This is the reality of the process of language: meaning-making is dialogic, unstable, and forever open to disruption, interruption, and fragmentation. (2004, 10–11)

Obviously, from a perspective of therapeutic effectiveness, a client's story must not be altered merely to satisfy a dominant discourse or more specifically another's sense of accuracy; it has to supply its own meaning. And, as my clients' accounts have amply demonstrated (despite numerous intrapersonal and social obstacles), they can and do supply meaning. My consistent experience has been that, in insisting that a client's story stand alone, we, the client and the therapist, eventually witness the birth of an internally constructed and regulated system of validity and self-worth that is remarkably reliable, despite the influence of a patriarchal discourse.

Ken Plummer provides a further perspective for conceptualizing, as research, this analysis of the narratives and the results that have grown out of my private practice. In offering a symbolic interactionist analysis of what he refers to as the 'pragmatic connection,' Plummer calls for pursuing other possible and non-traditional ways of valuing the narrative above and beyond a definition that has been externally produced and validated:

> The concern is less directly with truth, and more with matters of consequence: to consider the consequences of saying a particular story under particular circumstances. In this lies much of the power of story analysis. Stories help people to say certain things at certain times and in certain places, and likewise not to say them at others. Sexual stories can now be examined for the roles they play in lives, in contexts, in social order. (1995, 172)

Here, Plummer's insight into the power of the narrative, and its consequences, focuses on the interplay that occurs as a personal viewpoint is accepted or rejected by the social one. In turn, Martin Kohli's gaze, which has still more in common with my own work, is fixed on the interpersonal consequences of reading such stories. He suggests, 'One could say that an autobiographical narrative informs us about how the subject thematizes and constructs his own biography (in a given situation) and, by doing this, reaffirms (or even constitutes) his identity, and plans his actions' (1981, 70). In this sense, Kohli precedes me in establishing individual account construction by the client/teller/writer, 'an important topic in its own right,' as a pursuit worthy of research and provides additional support for the pragmatic value of narrative analysis.

Paul Thompson also offers a simple and most persuasive argument for those who might still dismiss the importance of the narrative genre:

> For the sociologist disillusioned with the crude mass empiricism of the quantitative survey, and the aggregating of masses of data abstracted from their sources in timeless, impersonal slices, the life history appears to offer information which is from its very nature coherent, rooted in real social experience, and is therefore capable of generating wholly fresh sociological insights as opposed to the self-reflecting answers of predetermined questions. (1981, 292)

As well, Daniel Bertaux in his discussion of the place of 'life stories' in sociological research expresses a point of view that supports not only Thompson's conclusion, but my own position, regarding the strength of narrative analysis: 'The concern with representativity of samples, with data analysis, with proof, can be met also with this reputedly 'qualitative' approach, and that this approach yields even more: a direct access to the level of social relations which constitute, after all, the very substance of sociological knowledge' (1981, 31).

Additional credence for this type of analysis comes again from Smith, who looks at the matter of account creation, though slightly differently. Her focus rests on the collective consequences of these individual constructions. It is her contention that 'each speaker from a new site discloses a new problematic for inquiry' (1987, 223). Together the problematic of each narrative amounts to what is an expansion of 'the consciousness of society from the standpoint of women' (223). The value of Smith's perspective comes, first, from within the gendered individual, then from what insight these experiences create collectively. Each account therefore stands as a considerable contribution in its own right. It is particularly upon this important premise that I rest my work. In short, strong arguments have been made for using the likes of the therapeutic sexual exploitation account as substantiation for sociological analyses.

No doubt other therapists have joined me in wondering if relaying sexual-exploitation accounts to an audience beyond the therapeutic environment is advisable. The threat of widespread invalidation or even a dismissal of the clients' experiences and understandings, combined with the public scrutiny they would endure, render this a risky endeavour. Since beginning this project, I have placed these concerns at the forefront. I remain sensitive to the issue of making public the accounts that my clients have entrusted to me to convey. In confronting this particular apprehension, I again found Dorothy Smith to be most helpful. She satisfactorily addresses the ethics of this concern in *The Everyday World as Problematic*:

> The fulcrum of a sociology for women is the standpoint of the subject. A sociology for women preserves the presence of subjects as knowers and actors. It does not transform subjects into the objects of study or make use of conceptual devices for eliminating the active presence of subjects. Its methods of thinking and its analytic procedures must preserve the presence of the active and experiencing subject. (1987, 105)

I position my clients here as 'knowers' and authors. Doing so has brought me to recognize that the greater damage would lie in not allowing the accounts to represent themselves. To investigate these abuse experiences from only a theoretical vantage point might promote further objectifications of the clients' experiences.

Finally, as my initial intent to transmit these accounts to an outside audience was beginning to be realized, I had a related but more personal doubt: I questioned my ability to communicate these stories and to relay them with any degree of accuracy. I recognize that I am hardly alone in either my attempt to locate an adequate perspective from which to relay someone else's story or in my consideration of her as an important source of sociological research. All of us who are engaged in research strain to get a handle on the authentic transmission of a story. Yet as Geertz writes, 'The burden of description, saying what it is others are saying is not so easily shed' (1983, 374). These words highlight the benefits of reflexiveness in this shared endeavour and applies equally well to me and to my clients in our efforts at account construction.

My merging of therapy and sociology was a move that, in part, came out of attempting to make greater sense of my clients' quests. I have served as an informed intermediary in introducing my clients' accounts into a broader discourse. My task has been to encourage further identity-reconstruction research in the field by taking these isolated accounts and situating them within social research, so that they may thereby be recognized as an important line of inquiry. The 'coming out' of the narrative into public view involved addressing problems for the client, and for myself, as therapist and as researcher. It involved moving from the individual's world to the social world, in order to more fully comprehend our discoveries in the context of reflexive therapy. It also entailed our exposing the nature, impact, and problems surrounding expressing the 'what' of sexual exploitation. This was a step that the clients who offered their narratives to this study greatly wanted to take.

In closing, social research has provided a means to express and understand my therapeutic findings. I have found corroboration in selective writings for what I have observed, in therapy, which extends beyond the private and subjective projections of client and therapist. These primarily theoretical studies on related social and cultural problems have lent credence to the therapeutic account as a sociological method, but most importantly, they have substantiated the purpose and influence of the content of these accounts. I am convinced of the importance and worth of these individual accounts. So too are my clients. They found in their narratives the genuineness, authority, and interconnectedness that they required and had pursued.

Conclusion: Mind, Body, and Society

The main purpose of this study has been to apply another field of inquiry, most predominantly sociology, to my clients' therapeutic accounts of sexual exploitation. Analytical therapy has traditionally placed its emphasis on the intrapersonal dimension of self-transformation. In contrast, sociology's principal focus has historically been on collective transformations. My interest, as a practising analytical therapist and professional sociologist, has been to explore the transformational space between the intrapersonal and the social experiences of self and of finding other ways of perceiving and presenting it. This dual perspective, a fresh way of seeing my clients, has contributed to sociological knowledge significant personal and collective experiences.

Early on in my practice, in my effort to better understand the process of account formation, I became interested in narrative therapy. The prevalence of interest in narrative signalled a valuable intellectual and social shift, beginning in the early 1980s, towards the situated and experiential. My attraction to this approach, simply put, lay in the notion that clients, after having so much taken from them through abuse, could be restored to a vital relationship with their past, by their own narrative production. Much of the narrative therapy was influenced by social research, borrowing, for example, from Foucault's (1980b) ideas about the power–knowledge relationship and Goffman's (1967) notions of interpretative frameworks. I nevertheless came to view its particular application, like many therapeutic methods, as quite formulaic and reductionist. In addition, it tended to stress cognitively oriented solutions, whereas my clients were seeking intuitive and holistic ones. In an attempt to capitalize on the regenerative quality that these and other approaches seemed to offer, neither my clients nor I remained entirely loyal to any one approach. In fact, the success of my clients' self-reparations depended upon our unremitting reconsideration and reinterpretation of our methods. It necessitated also our continual renegotiation of the accounts before us, as clients introduced their own unique associations and metaphors.

In seeking to give credence to both the internal and external dimensions of my clients' experiences, I adopted an approach in counselling that I call reflexive therapy. This approach has been borne out of a combined therapeutic and sociological interest and a definition of reflexivity that is generally shared by both disciplines. Initially, I did not regard my clients' communications of trauma as either 'stories' or 'narratives,' but rather as 'accounts,' although they are now terms that I feel compelled to employ because it is within these models/theories/categories that my clients' experiences are best described. These terms were objectifications that gradually seeped into the therapeutic and sociological discourses much like 'survivor' had generally come to dominate the sexual-abuse discourse of the last decade. I viewed them as useful designations that I guardedly yet increasingly allowed to pervade my therapeutic approach.

In my early days as a therapist I noted that a great many of my clients underwent change during the course of personal account construction that deeply affected them intrapersonally and socially. We explored ways of giving expression, in words, to these seemingly indescribable transformations. Through this work, I also increasingly came to appreciate the extent to which variable public perspectives and discourse on the phenomenon of sexual abuse influenced and even defined my clients' relationships to their own accounts. My research therefore began with an awakening to the process and significance of the therapeutic and social interaction, and this, in turn, has led to this study. Together, these chapters and the accounts have attempted to provide specific insights into the nature and impact of sexual exploitation. They shed light on how the narrative construction defines self-identity. As well, they address the power of the dominant discourse to characterize and define such private experiences and thus alert us to the danger that if such externally imposed definitions are not made fully conscious, the integrative process of 'the self' will be impeded. These private concerns are therefore public issues.

My clients laboured in and outside of therapy to interject their own perspectives into what we recognized as externally imposed a priori public scripts that insisted on representing them. Ultimately, for them, individual revision, not social labelling, proved to be the most powerful and self-sustaining method of attaining authenticity and ultimate healing. I came to agree with Denzin's comment that 'persons are the best observers of their selves and can tell stories that accurately reflect their lives' (1992, 90). In doing so, clients reconstructed their own narratives and situated them in their life, granting them a prominence and form that their abuses had formerly assumed. I argue that it is the client's deliberate shift in perspective, in progressing from an inherited script to establishing authority over the words and meanings that represent her, where the significance of our therapeutic work lies. I also hold that the clients' reclamation of personal validity, and the research implications that such processes suggest for sociologists and therapists, is complex and can ultimately be established only through micro studies with identity formation.

The stages of their reintegration and self-acceptance become evident as each account is begun, reworked, and concluded. Such reintegrative work inevitably encompassed internal, external, unconscious, conscious, social, cultural, and embodied aspects of self. Different dimensions of my clients' therapeutic accounts have been emphasized throughout. Collectively, these narratives demonstrate private and isolated attempts at a reunification with a personal identity from which they have become estranged or never knew. By insights derived from dream work, magnified moments associated with memory fragments, and other sources documented throughout this work, my clients' strategies demonstrate a departure from pre-therapeutic, socially constructed descriptions of their experiences.

Specifically, chapter 2, 'Locating the Self: The Language of Survival,' explored through one representative story the perceptions of a great many of my clients who needed to define themselves independently amid powerful, external, and collective attempts to characterize them and their experiences of sexual exploitation in particular ways. This study demonstrated that if the client is genuinely to express personally rendered insights, she must be aware of the pervasive character of textually mediated constructions. In this sense the presence of dominant and authoritative social constructions affecting my client's experiences is of both therapeutic and sociological concern.

What followed in chapter 3, 'Anguish, Dreams, and Remembering: The Reflexive Process,' was a concentrated reflexive analysis of this turning inward, of finding metaphors and understandings ample enough to encompass destructive and life-altering experiences. It explained why, when revisiting a reality of atrocious exploitations, a client may initially prefer to cling to a fragmented and painful yet largely superficial understanding of her experience. She does this in an effort to avoid a potentially deeper and even more painful delving into what had been done to her. Yet through a reflexive exploration and in a growing awareness of her multilayered isolation, the client often calls upon previously unrecognized personal sources to extract and familiarize herself with the very source of her pain. This is undertaken in an effort to repair a fragmented self, establish a reconnection to her social world, and in so doing, to fully rejoin a wider circle of significant relationships. This chapter explains the interconnectedness of intrapersonal experiences and sociological theory, through reflexive transformation, the process of stepping outside of oneself to see oneself. It illustrates as well how social research provides the means for translating to a non-therapeutic audience a highly subjective experience.

The symbolic nature of our therapeutic communications and the importance of perceiving and understanding clients' tentative and veiled expressions are key elements in a world where they otherwise go unseen. Those were explored more deeply in chapter 4, 'From Silence to Narration: Exposing and Interpreting a Fragmented Self.' In emphasizing the difficulty of conveying an account, I pointed clearly to the importance of a hermeneutic understanding of the process, of examining the communication of a story in its entirety, in order to make sense of what is being said. This private world contains intensely personal material that only therapy can mediate, but that sociology can help to elucidate. Sociological explanations were essential, for example, in making sense of the client's desire to speak despite a multitude of good reasons for her to remain silent. The underlying intensity and importance of the client's longing for a social reflection of her intrapersonal trauma was made clearer and more understandable within a sociological framework.

Contradictions between intrapersonal and public demands for validity and the sometimes very evident collective unwillingness to believe claims of sexual abuse have often negated a client's perspective on what has happened to her and can seriously shake her certainty of her own experience. My final chapter, 'Private Worlds, Public Worlds, and the Pursuit of Certainty,' looked at the distinct issues that surround internal and external validation and, in particular, those obstacles that impede the free and public expression of deeply private stories. The narrative, as I learned first-hand through my clients' pursuits and in later gathering relevant sociological material, is ultimately a self-verifying enterprise. As Richard Sennett has argued, 'The psyche dwells in a state of endlessly becoming – a selfhood which is never finished' (1998, 133). My work with these accounts, I recognize, has focused on relatively brief periods in a lengthy and ceaseless production of the self. Whether or not these narratives represent any ultimate 'truth' is of course largely a moot point.

Overall, then, my clients' therapeutic chronicles of sexual exploitation have illuminated several key points that align and enhance sociological and therapeutic interpretations of self-perception and self-presentation. They have shown that the social understanding of their experience alters their private interpretation. Accordingly, one finding that strongly resonates throughout this work is that private and public interpretations need to be considered together because their influences on the individual are inseparable. My clients have demonstrated this point powerfully again and again as many initially struggled to make their accounts fit an external standard of validity that did little more than accentuate their self-doubts – a product of fragmented memories, family denial of their experience, and their own diminished sense of self-authority. This interrelationship has been illustrated repeatedly if only by the strength of my clients' desire to speak and re-establish a significant social connection. Their desire is ultimately so powerful as to override any fears of exposing long-held secrets, of being disbelieved, or of being held responsible for what has happened to them.

This inquiry has further demonstrated the need for enhanced therapeutic awareness, of how the imposition of prevailing interpretations, including those existing in popular self-help literature, affect the client to the point of shutting down her creative capacity for self-interpretation. Simultaneously, it makes the point that a momentary freeing from external discourses fosters a crucial and necessary sense of agency for the client. By means of a reflexive perspective, my clients were enabled to disentangle themselves from popular explanations and develop an internal perspective that was 'true' to them.

The clients' symbols are shaped by a collective language and then individually interpreted, reflected, sometimes reinterpreted, and then applied in order to substantiate their experience. Clients know when symbols truly represent their experience. The magnified moment that its exactitude produces resonates for them at all levels of their being. Our reflexive approach considers the relationship between the dimensions of the client's self as one that cannot be wholly understood in isolation from the others. The reflexive narrative process draws the clients' self-generated symbols into its cycle of reflected comprehensions. They are in turn used to encapsulate and explain the clients' traumas to themselves and others for the first time.

This study also shows how the value of these accounts stems partially from their local quality. Theorizing allows us to see broadly but does not always permit us to see intimately. The micro study is a perspective that social research cannot afford to circumvent. The power and immediacy of my clients' narratives supports Smith's insistence that women's research has to be conducted within the experience one is seeking to describe (Smith 1987), for this is where women's lives unfold. In addition, these narratives affirm Smith's now widely shared view that women have remained outside of the powerful dialogues that shape their existence. This insight, in turn, offers a vital sociological explanation for my clients' struggles, as women, towards self-acceptance and expression.

These constructions were initially beyond my clients' abilities to assimilate. As a therapist, I could mediate these constructions; as a sociologist, I could socially integrate and amplify them. The heart of this process required perpetual ingenuity from each of us, out of which developed a transformation of perception. This took the form first of the clients' changing view of themselves and second of my perspectives about them and their social world in the context of their intrapersonal experiences of sexual abuse. In bridging private and social aspects of experience to foster self-reparation, my clients' accounts demonstrate the importance of moving towards integration at all experiential levels.

These findings have been consistently observed in my participation in the creation of hundreds of sexual-exploitation accounts over the last fifteen years and more. They address social themes that need to be further linked to wider social and cultural theories and research. Some sociological theory to date has prepared a space into which such local, subjective, symbolic, and intrapersonal work on the self may flow. In this regard, Burkitt's (1999) discussion of the body as soul and his exploration of the inseparable dimensions of self come closest to opening up analysis in this area. Rose's inquiry into 'practices of subjectification' (1996, 186) and 'narratives of feeling' (1989, 248) overlap, as well. But more theoretical and empirical work clearly needs to be done.

This project of conducting research from the perspective of a therapeutic practice has also produced insights, questions, and implications for future research and practice. From a combined sociological and

therapeutic vantage point I see, for example, the need for further ampli-
fying my clients' use of symbols as a dual medium for understanding
and communicating their experiences of self while simultaneously
buffering their emerging self from the scrutiny of others. This application of the symbol as a method of communication uniquely bridges the
subjective and intrapersonal world with a symbolically interactive
social world and warrants further study.

I have also worked to address through narrated accounts of sexual-
abuse experiences the interconnectedness between the intrapersonal
and social worlds of sexual-abuse victims, as revealed in reflexive therapy. Nikolas Rose eloquently states what I now well understand as
therapist/participant observer/ethnographer, which I have attempted
to demonstrate in this study:

> Although we are, no doubt, neither at the dawn of a new age nor at the
> ending of an old one, we can, perhaps, begin to discern the cracking of this
> once secure place of interiority, the disconnecting of some of the lines that
> have made up this diagram, the possibility that, if we cannot disinvent
> ourselves, we might at least enhance the contestability of the forms of
> being that have been invented for us, and begin to invent ourselves differ-
> ently. (1996, 197)

In the writing of this book I have come to strongly appreciate that the
therapeutic exchange yields vital social insights and must not be left as
a closed form of communication. Just as the client needs to reach reflexively, both inside and outside of herself, for fresh insights and feedback,
so too must the therapist and the sociologist reach more deeply inside
and beyond their accustomed disciplinary realms.

References

Anderson, Harlene, and Harold A. Goolishian. 1988. Human systems as linguistic systems: Preliminary and evolving ideas about the implications for clinical theory. *Family Process* 27 (4): 371–93.

Archdiocese of St John's. 1990. *The report of the Archdiocesan Commission of Inquiry into the Sexual Abuse of Children by members of the clergy.* 2 vols. St John's: Archdiocese of St John's.

Bagley, Chris. 1986. Mental health and the in-family sexual abuse of children and adolescents. In *Sexual abuse of children in the 1980s: Ten essays and an annotated bibliography,* ed. Benjamin Schlesinger, 30–50. Toronto: University of Toronto Press.

Barr, Marleen S., and Richard Feldstein, eds. 1989. *Discontented discourses: feminism / textual intervention / psychoanalysis.* Urbana: University of Illinois Press.

Bart, Pauline B., and Eileen Geil Morgan, eds. 1993. *Violence against women: The bloody footprints.* London: Sage.

Bass, Ellen, and Laura Davis. 1988. *The courage to heal.* New York: Harper and Row.

Beckett, Samuel. 1965. *Three novels by Samuel Beckett.* New York: Grove.

Berger, Peter, and Thomas Luckmann. 1966. *The social construction of reality.* New York: Doubleday.

Bertaux, Daniel, ed. 1981. *Biography and society.* Newbury Park: Sage.

Bettelheim, Bruno. 1979. *Surviving and other essays.* New York: Knopf.

Bolker, Joan. 1995. Forgetting ourselves. *Readings* 10 (2):12–15.

Brownmiller, Susan. 1975. *Against our will: Men, women and rape.* New York: Simon and Schuster.

Bruner, Edward. 1997. Ethnography as narrative. In *Memory, identity, commu-*

nity: The idea of narrative in the human sciences, eds. Lewis P. Hinchman and Sandra K. Hinchman, 264–80. Albany: State University of New York Press.

Bruner, Jerome. 1987. Life as narrative. *Social Research* 54 (1): 11–32.

Burgess, Ann, Nicholas Groth, Lytle Holstrom, and Suzanne Sgroi. 1985. *Sexual assault of children and adolescents*. Lexington, MA: Lexington Books.

Burkitt, Ian. 1999. *Bodies of thought*. London: Sage.

Carey, James W. 1989. *Communication as culture: Essays on media and society.* New York. Routledge.

Catani, Maurizio. 1981. Social life history as ritualized oral exchange. In *Biography and society*, ed. Daniel Bertaux, 211–24. London: Sage.

Cornell, William. F. 1995. A plea for a measure of ambiguity. *Readings* 10 (2): 4–12.

Denzin, Norman K. 1989. *Interpretive biography.* Newbury Park: Sage.

– 1992. *Symbolic interactionism and cultural studies*. Cambridge, MA: Blackwell.

Des Pres, Terrence. 1980. *The survivor: An anatomy of life in the death camp*. New York: Oxford University Press.

Douglas, Mary. 1966. *Purity and danger*. London: Routledge Kegan and Paul.

Elliot, Jane. 2005. *Using narrative in social research*. London: Sage.

Ellis, Jan. 1990. The therapeutic journey: A guide for travelers. In *Healing voices*, ed. Toni Ann Laidlaw and Cheryl Malmo, 243–71. San Francisco: Jossey-Bass.

Engel, Beverley. 1989. *The right to innocence*. Los Angeles: Tarcher.

Featherstone, M., Mike Hepworth, and Bryan Turner, eds. 1991. *The body*. London: Sage.

Finkelhor, David. 1984. *Child sexual abuse: New theory and research*. New York: Free Press.

– 1986. *Impact of child sexual abuse: A review of the research*. Ottawa: Minister of Supply and Services.

– 1989. *New myths about child sexual abuse*. Ottawa: Minister of Supply and Services.

Finney, Lynne D. 1992. *Reach for the rainbow*. New York: Putnam.

Foucault, Michel. 1972. *The archaeology of knowledge*. London: Tavistock.

– 1980a. *The history of sexuality*. Vol. 1, *An introduction*. New York: Vintage Books.

– 1980b. *Power/knowledge: Selected interviews and other writings, 1972–77*. Ed. Colin Gordon. Brighton, Sussex: Harvester.

Frank, Arthur W. 1991. For a sociology of the body: An analytical review. In *The body: Social process and cultural theory*, ed. Mike Featherstone, Mike Hepworth, and Bryan S. Turner, 36–102. Thousand Oaks, CA: Sage.

Frankl, Victor. 1959. *Man's search for meaning*. New York: Simon and Schuster.

Freund, Peter E.S. 1990. The expressive body: A common ground for the sociology of emotions and health and illness. *Sociology of Health and Illness* 12 (4): 452–77.

Gagnon, Nicole. 1981. On the analysis of life accounts. In *Biography and society*, ed. Daniel Bertraux, 47–60. London: Sage.

Geertz, Clifford. 1983. *Local knowledge*. New York: Basic Books.

Giddens, Anthony. 1991. *Modernity and self-identity*. Cambridge, UK: Polity.

Gilligan, Carol. 1982. *In a different voice*. Cambridge, MA: Harvard University Press.

– 2002. *The birth of pleasure: A new map of love*. New York: Vintage Books.

Goffman, Erving. 1959. *The presentation of self in everyday life*. New York: Doubleday Anchor.

– 1963. *Stigma*. Englewood Cliffs: Prentice-Hall.

– 1967. *Interaction ritual*. New York: Doubleday Anchor.

Goldstein, Diane E. 2004. *Once upon a virus: Aids legends and vernacular risk perception*. Logan, UT: Utah State University Press.

Hankiss, Agnes. 1981. Ontologies of the self: On the mythological rearranging of one's life history. In *Biography and society*, ed. Daniel Bertaux, 203–10. London: Sage.

Harris, Michael. 1990. *Unholy orders: Tragedy at Mount Cashel*. New York: Viking Penguin.

Hartsock, Nancy. 1987. The feminist standpoint: Developing the ground for specifically feminist historical materialism. In *Feminism and methodology*, ed. Sandra Harding, 157–80. Indiana: Indiana University Press.

Hartsock, Nancy. 1998. *The feminist standpoint revisited and other essays*. Boulder, CO: Westview.

Haugaard, Jeffrey J., and N. Dickon Reppucci. 1989. *The sexual abuse of children*. San Francisco: Jossey-Bass.

Hepworth, Mike, and Bryan S. Turner. 1982. *Confessions*. London: Routledge and Kegan Paul.

Herman, Judith Lewis. 1992. *Trauma and recovery*. New York: Basic Books.

Hinchman, Lewis P., and Sandra K. Hinchman, eds. 1997. *Memory, identity, community: The idea of narrative in the human sciences*. Albany: SUNY Press.

Hochschild, Arlie Russell. 1983. *The managed heart: Commercialization of human feeling*. Berkeley: University of California Press.

Hughes, S.H.S. 1991. *The Royal Commission of Inquiry into the Response of the Newfoundland Criminal Justice System to Complaints*. 2 vols. St John's: Office of the Queen's Printer.

Jung, C.G. 1958. *Psyche and symbol*. New York: Doubleday Anchor.

– 1974. *Dreams*. Princeton: Princeton University Press.

Kelly, Liz. 1988a. *Surviving sexual violence*. Cambridge: Polity.

– 1988b. What's in a name? Defining child sexual abuse. *Feminist Review* 28 (January): 65–73.

Klapp, Orrin. 1991. *Inflation of symbols*. New Brunswick: Transaction.

Kogan, Steven M., and Anita C. Brown. 1998. Reading against the lines: Resisting foreclosure in therapy discourse. *Family Process* 37 (4): 495–512.

Kohli, Martin. 1981. Biography: Account, text, method. In *Biography and society*, ed. Daniel Bertraux, 61–76. London: Sage.

Kunzman, Kristin A. 1990. *The healing way*. San Francisco: Harper and Row.

Lacan, Jacques. 1990. *Television: A challenge to the psychoanalytic establishment*. Ed. J. Copjec, trans. J. Mehlman. New York: Norton.

Lasch, Christopher. 1984. *The minimal self*. New York: Norton.

Lemert, Charles. 2002. *Social things: An introduction to the sociological life*. Lanham, MD: Rowman and Littlefield.

Maines, David R. 1993. Narrative's moment and sociology's phenomena: Toward a narrative sociology. *Sociological Quarterly* 34 (1): 17–37.

Mead, George H. 1934. *Mind, self, and society*. Chicago: University of Chicago Press.

Mills, C.W. 1959. *The sociological imagination*. Oxford: Oxford University Press.

Myerhoff, Barbara. 1992. *Remembered lives*. Ann Arbor: University of Michigan Press.

Newman, Elana. 2004. Narrative, gender, and recovery from childhood sexual abuse. In *Survivor rhetoric: Negotiations and narrativity in abused women's language*, ed. Christine Shearer-Cremean and Carol L. Winklemann, 23–41. Toronto: University of Toronto Press.

Orr, Elaine Neil. 1987. *Tillie Olsen and a feminist spiritual vision*. Jackson: University Press of Mississippi.

Pearce, Joseph Chilton. 1992. *Evolution's end: Claiming the potential of our intellect*. San Francisco: Harper.

Penn, Peggy. 1998. Rape flashbacks: Constructing a new narrative. *Family Process* 37 (3): 299–310.

Pharr, Suzanne. 1997. Homophobia as a weapon of sexism. In *The social construction of difference and inequality: Race, class, gender and sexuality*, ed. Tracey E. Ore, 501–10. Boston: McGraw Hill.

Plummer, Ken. 1995. *Telling sexual stories*. London: Routledge.

Reno, Janet. 1990. *Ishmael alone survived*. London: Bucknell University Press.

Ricoeur, Paul. 1967. *The symbolism of evil*. New York: Beacon.

– 1984. *Time and narrative*. Chicago: University of Chicago Press.

Rogers, Rix G. 1992. *Reaching solutions: The report of the special advisor to the min-*

ister of national Health and Welfare on Child Sexual Abuse in Canada. Ottawa: Minister of Supply and Services.

Rose, Nikolas. 1989. *Governing the soul: The shaping of the private self.* London: Routledge.

– 1996. *Inventing ourselves: Psychology, power, and personhood.* Cambridge: Cambridge University Press.

Rowbotham, Sheila. 1973. *Woman's consciousness, man's world.* Middlesex: Penguin Books.

Sanford, John A. 1978. *Dreams and healing.* New York: Paulist.

Scarry, Elaine. 1985. *The body in pain.* Oxford: Oxford University Press.

Schlesinger, Benjamin, ed. 1986. *Sexual abuse of children in the 1980s.* Toronto: University of Toronto Press.

Seligman, Adam. 1997. *The problem of trust.* Princeton: Princeton University Press.

Sennett, Richard. 1998. *The corrosion of character.* New York: Norton.

Shearer-Cremean, Christine, and Carol L. Winklemann, eds. 2004. *Survivor rhetoric: Negotiations and narrativity in abused women's language.* Toronto: University of Toronto Press.

Simmel, Georg. 1971. The stranger. In *Georg Simmel on individuality and social forms,* ed. Donald N. Levine, 143–9. Heritage of Sociology Series. Chicago: University of Chicago Press.

Smith, Dorothy E. 1987. *The everyday world as problematic.* Toronto: University of Toronto Press.

– 1990a. *The conceptual practices of power.* Toronto: University of Toronto Press.

– 1990b. K is mentally ill. In Smith, *Texts, facts and femininity: Exploring the relations of ruling,* 12–52. London: Routledge.

– 1990c. *Texts, facts, and femininity: Exploring the relations of ruling.* London: Routledge.

– 1999. *Writing the social.* Toronto: University of Toronto Press.

Stanko, Elizabeth. 1990. *Everyday violence.* London: Pandora.

Stanley, Liz. 1990. *Feminist praxis: Research, theory and epistemology in feminist sociology.* London: Routledge.

Stearns, Maurice A., ed. 1974. *Perspectives on Newfoundland society and culture.* St John's: Institute for Social and Economic Research, Memorial University.

Stevens, Wallace. 1982. *The collected poems of Wallace Stevens.* New York: Vintage Books.

Strictling, Bonnell Lewis. 1990. Reclaiming the inner child: Jungian dream analysis. In *Healing Voices,* ed. Toni Ann Laidlaw and Cheryl Malmo, 143–60. San Francisco: Jossey-Bass.

Thompson, Paul. 1981. Life histories and the analysis of social change. In *Biography and Society*, ed. Daniel Bertaux, 289–306. London: Sage.

Tomm, Karl. 1987. Interventive interviewing: Part 2; Reflexive questioning as a means to enable self healing. *Family Process* 26 (2): 167–83.

Turner, Victor. 1967. *The forest of symbols*. London: Cornell University Press.

Vella, Susan. 1992. False memory syndrome: The latest defense to childhood claims. *Jurisfemme* 12 (4): 1–2.

Weinbaum, Batya. 2004. A survivor within a culture of survivors: Untangling the language of sexual abuse in oral history narrative collected in a politically violent situation. In *Survivor rhetoric: Negotiations and narrativity in abused women's language*, ed. Christine Shearer-Cremean and Caroline L. Winkle-mann, 64–93. Toronto: University of Toronto Press.

White, Michael, and David Epston. 1990. *Narrative means to therapeutic ends*. Adelaide: Dulwich.

Wiesel, Elie. 1990. *From the kingdom of memory*. New York: Summit Books.

Wolf, Naomi. 1991. *The beauty myth*. New York: Morrow.

Woodman, Marion. 1982. *Addiction to perfection*. Toronto: Inner City Books.

– 1990. *The ravaged bridegroom*. Toronto: Inner City Books.

Index